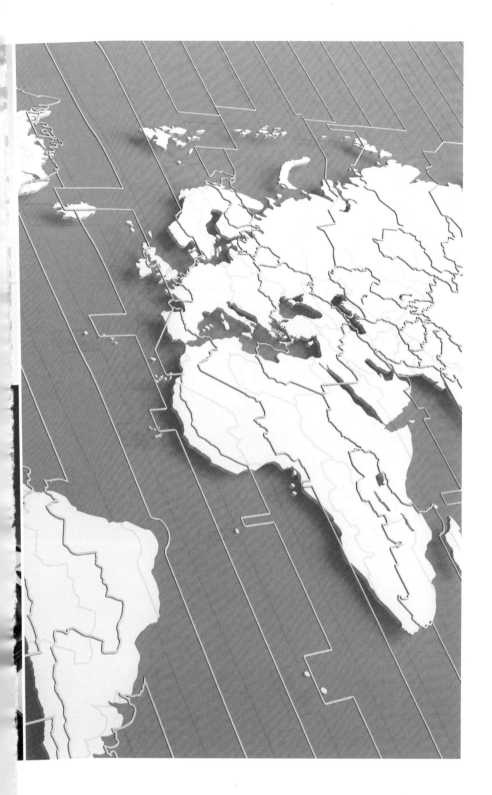

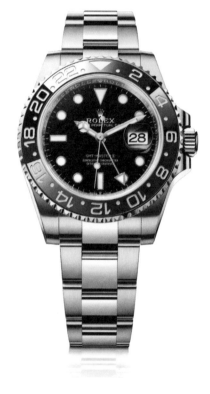

OYSTER PERPETUAL GMT-MASTER II

ROLEX

Van Cleef & Arpels

Haute Joaillerie, place Vendôme since 1906

**Rubis flamboyant
transformable necklace**
White and pink gold, diamonds,
one cushion-cut ruby of 25.76 carats,
18 oval-cut and cushion-cut rubies
for 30.40 carats.

PARACHUTE

Wonderfully cozy home essentials.

danish design by · made by

LINDBERG

Premium
Subscription

Become a Premium Subscriber for $75 per year, and you'll receive four
print issues of the magazine and full access to our online archives, plus a
set of *Kinfolk* notecards and a wide range of special offers.

KINFOLK

FOUNDER & CREATIVE DIRECTOR
Nathan Williams

EDITOR-IN-CHIEF
John Clifford Burns

EDITOR
Harriet Fitch Little

ART DIRECTOR - PRINT
Christian Møller Andersen

DESIGN DIRECTOR
Alex Hunting

COPY EDITOR
Rachel Holzman

BRAND DIRECTOR
Amy Woodroffe

COMMERCIAL DIRECTOR
Mads Westendahl

COMMUNICATIONS DIRECTOR
Jessica Gray

DESIGNER & ART DIRECTOR
Staffan Sundström

PRODUCER
Cecilie Jegsen

SALES & DISTRIBUTION DIRECTOR
Edward Mannering

STUDIO MANAGER
Susanne Buch Petersen

EDITORIAL ASSISTANTS
Gabriele Dellisanti
Natalia Lauritzen

CONTRIBUTING EDITORS
Michael Anastassiades
Jonas Bjerre-Poulsen
Ilse Crawford
Margot Henderson
Leonard Koren
Hans Ulrich Obrist
Amy Sall
Matt Willey

WORDS
Alex Anderson
Rima Sabina Aouf
Ellie Violet Bramley
Katie Calautti
James Clasper
Stephanie d'Arc Taylor
Daphnée Denis
Alix Fox
Bella Gladman
Nikolaj Hansson
Alexandra Heminsley
Tim Hornyak
Robert Ito
Ana Kinsella
Scarlett Lindeman
Megan Nolan
Debika Ray
Elizabeth Sankey
Rhian Sasseen
Charles Shafaieh
Komal Sharma
Ben Shattuck
Stevie Mackenzie-Smith
Pip Usher
Annick Weber

CROSSWORD
Anna Gundlach

PUBLICATION DESIGN
Alex Hunting Studio

COVER PHOTOGRAPH
Romain Laprade

PHOTOGRAPHY
Gustav Almestål
Victoria Barmak
Ted Belton
Claire Cottrell
Pelle Crépin
Iringó Demeter
Brooke DiDonato
Ingrid Fetell Lee
Antonio Guerreiro
Victoria Ivanova
Cecilie Jegsen
Trevor King
Romain Laprade
Fanny Latour-Lambert
Emma Le Doyen
Salva López
Katie McCurdy
Christian Møller Andersen
Emman Montalvan
Renzo Navarro
Jorge Perez Ortiz
Elena Seibert
Alexandre Souêtre
Aaron Tilley

STYLING, HAIR & MAKEUP
Ashley Abtahie
Matilda Beckman
Taan Doan
Hirokazu Endo
Zidjian Floro
Fleet Ilya
Jardine Hammond
Niklas Hansen
Helena Kastensson
Pernilla Löfberg
Katie Mellinger
Yohey Nakatsuka
David Nolan
Mike O'Gorman
Martin Persson
Nadia Pizzimenti
Sandy Suffield
Camille-Joséphine Teisseire
Ronnie Tremblay
Nicole Wittman

ISSUE 34
Kinfolk (ISSN 2596-6154) is published quarterly by Ouur ApS, Amagertorv 14, 1, 1160 Copenhagen, Denmark. Printed by Taylor Bloxham Limited in Leicester, United Kingdom. Color reproduction by PH Media in Roche, United Kingdom. All rights reserved. No part of this publication may be reproduced, distributed or transmitted in any form or by any means, including photocopying or other electronic or mechanical methods, without prior written permission of the editor-in-chief, except in the case of brief quotations embodied in critical reviews and certain other noncommercial uses permitted by copyright law. The US annual subscription price is $87 USD. Airfreight and mailing in the USA by Worldnet Shipping Inc., 156-15, 146th Avenue, 2nd Floor, Jamaica, NY 11434, USA. Application to mail at periodicals postage prices is pending at Jamaica NY 11431. US Postmaster: send address changes to Kinfolk, Worldnet Shipping Inc., 156-15, 146th Avenue, 2nd Floor, Jamaica, NY 11434, USA. Subscription records are maintained at Ouur ApS, Amagertorv 14, 1, 1160 Copenhagen, Denmark.

info@kinfolk.com
www.kinfolk.com

Published by Ouur Media
Amagertorv 14, Level 1
1160 Copenhagen, Denmark

The views expressed in Kinfolk magazine are those of the respective contributors and are not necessarily shared by the company or its staff.

SUBSCRIBE
Kinfolk is published four times a year. To subscribe, visit kinfolk.com/subscribe or email us at info@kinfolk.com

CONTACT US
If you have questions or comments, please write to us at info@kinfolk.com. For advertising inquiries, get in touch at advertising@kinfolk.com. For partnerships and business opportunities, contact mads@kinfolk.com

A new perspective on tiles

Design by Edward Barber & Jay Osgerby,
Ronan & Erwan Bouroullec, Konstantin Grcic,
Raw Edges, Hella Jongerius, Inga Sempé,
Patricia Urquiola, Tokujin Yoshioka.

mutina.it

HOUSE OF
FINN JUHL

finnjuhl.com

PELICAN CHAIR 1940
BY FINN JUHL

HFJ

Issue 34

Welcome

Intimacy is what distinguishes those who are dear to us from those who are simply near. Perhaps you have found a moment of solitude in which to begin reading *Kinfolk*'s Intimacy Issue, but equally likely you are snatching time on a busy commute or escaping from the whirl of a hectic household. If so, flip first to our photo essay *Close Enough* on page 124 to find solace in Ted Belton's humorous portrayal of the many scenarios in which closeness can feel like a curse.

This issue of *Kinfolk* explores the balance between our contradictory cravings for both secure and stable relationships and the freedom to follow our hearts, our sexual desires, and our need to be whole without the help of another. We take psychotherapist Esther Perel as our lodestar. It's a role she's played for the clients at her New York practice and for millions of others through her books and the podcast *Where Should We Begin*, which offers the chance to listen in on anonymous couples during therapy sessions. Perel's approach has always been to challenge the fundamental contradictions in how we think about romantic intimacy: Is it really feasible to expect one person to fulfill our every need—for the rest of our life?

Following Perel's unconventional lead, our dive into intimacy focuses on appreciating the unusual corners in which it can flourish. In a long-form essay, Stephanie d'Arc Taylor talks to experts including advice columnist Dan Savage about the brave new world of ethical nonmonogamy. On page 170, we meet Resha Sharma and Ilya Fleet, who at first blush may appear to be a conventional married couple, but whose understanding of intimacy is tempered by the fact they run an erotic leatherwear company together. "We challenge each other in a way that we wouldn't in a platonic partnership," Sharma explains.

As anyone who has been told by a loved one, therapist or disgruntled ex that they need to spend some time "getting to know themselves" will attest, intimacy can also be experienced alone. Lori Gottlieb, a psychotherapist well-versed in listening to the stories of her clients, explains that the key to a better relationship with ourselves lies in the ability to edit our own narratives: "It's also about getting to un-know yourself," she says. Elsewhere, a photo essay by Gustav Almestål explores the solitary indulgence of comfort foods, so tied to our most intimate of spaces—our homes—and so appealing during break ups. We also celebrate the legacy of novelist Jackie Collins—whose bawdy tales of love and lust in Hollywood came to feel like sustaining relationships to many intimacy-starved readers.

In Issue Thirty-Four, we experience the thrill of people and places spilling their secrets. Amaryllis Fox—an ex-CIA spy who spent her 20s negotiating in some of the world's most dangerous conflict zones—cracks open the mysteries of the Clandestine Service, and what they've taught her about peace. On page 98, we present the result of our own months-long international operation: To gain access to an art deco royal palace in Gujurat, India.

As the nights close in, our contributors look beyond this world and into other more mysterious ones: They mull over the popularity of horoscopes and what to eat at funerals. For our cover shoot, photographer Romain Laprade explores the white orb of a modernist church that might well be the moon of a new planet.

JOHN CLIFFORD BURNS & HARRIET FITCH LITTLE

"When we return, that's where all our love lies."
MIRA BA – P.109

Photograph: Salva López

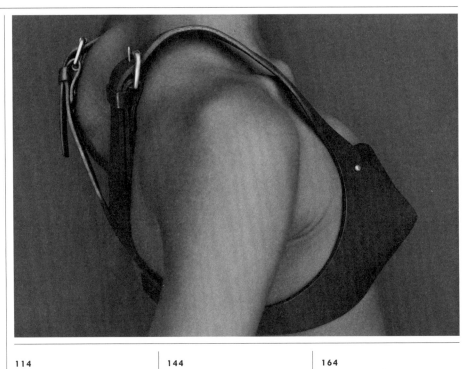
"Sometimes submitting is the most powerful thing. It's freeing."
RESHA SHARMA — P.174

Photograph: Iringó Demeter

1
Starters

TIM HORNYAK

How to Rekindle a Friendship

On inching closer when you've grown apart.

Friendships are vital to our health and well-being. Researchers at Michigan State University analyzed responses from over 270,000 people in nearly 100 countries and concluded that as we age, friendships are more influential than family ties in their effect on our health and happiness. Other studies have found that our immune systems and longevity benefit from strong social ties. And yet we don't have anything like a user manual for something so important—and fragile. Bonds forged over decades can easily fracture and even shatter, turning BFFs into strangers. Then, like a distant relative, an old friend can reappear, hoping to become part of your life again.

Whether and how to rekindle a friendship is a knotty issue. It's harder to form friendships as we get older; science also tells us that our social connections peak around age 25. For older adults, when a former buddy wants to enter our lives again, it may seem like too much of a bother, especially when family and work commitments take up most of our time. It's no surprise that there's a plethora of popular how-to books on threading the friendship maze, with titles like *The Friendship Fix*, *The Friendship Factor* and *Stop Being Lonely*.

From an early age, we tend to idealize friendships. Our parents and peers tell us about best friends and soul mates. The latter concept seems to descend from Aristotle, who defined friends as one soul inhabiting two bodies. This romantic notion was long-lived, with Oliver Goldsmith describing friendship in the 18th century as "disinterested commerce between equals" and Byron later rhapsodizing about it being "love without his wings!" After the Industrial Revolution, the thrill was gone. "Friendships begin with liking or gratitude—roots that can be pulled up," George Eliot wrote in 1876. Fellow English author Norman Douglas noted: "To find a friend one must close one eye. To keep him—two." Or as the French would say, *L'amour est aveugle; l'amitié ferme les yeux*; lovers may be blind, but friends close their eyes for each other.

When reconnecting, this idea of accepting friends along with all their foibles is worth remembering. A rekindled friendship can revive shared interests and histories, but we also have to consider that people and their needs change over time; a relationship that was effortless in the past may now need a bit more time and care to thrive.

Being communicative about your feelings and needs is the first step in your new journey with an old friend. With any luck, you'll be like Humphrey Bogart and Claude Rains in *Casablanca*, metaphorically walking off into the mist toward (another) beautiful friendship.

Unless you're exceptionally time-rich, it's worth holding on to the close friends you already have. It typically takes around 200 hours of shared activities and conversation before an acquaintance becomes a best friend.

Photograph: Emma Le Doyen

ANA KINSELLA

Last Supper

What to eat at a funeral.

In the midst of grief, food can often be the furthest thing from our minds. But for *Olivia Potts*, it was a humble banana cake that lifted her spirits in the days after her mother's death. Returning to London after the funeral, the then-24-year-old barrister was eating a lunch of leftovers on the train when she realized the comfort that food can bring in times of turmoil. In the weeks that followed, she took up cooking for the first time, baking cakes at home after work. The methodical certainty that came with following a recipe was a soothing balm. Soon she had traded the courts for studies at Le Cordon Bleu and today, six years later, Potts works as a writer and wedding caterer, with *A Half Baked Idea*, her memoir on grief and cake, published in July 2019.

Photograph: Victoria Ivanova

Here, she explains why we rely on food in times of grief, and the best foods to serve at a funeral.

AK: *What do you think the role of food is at a funeral?* **OP:** Before my mother's funeral, we did a funeral tasting—like a wedding tasting. It was about as weird as you'd imagine: me, my sister and my dad, a few days after Mum had died, when you're so mired in grief you have no idea what you're doing. We sat around this little table and were given different options. My family lives in the northeast of England, near the coast, and the caterer was offering little pots of shellfish—cockles and mussels and so on. My mum had a really bad allergy to shellfish. We were thinking: "Well, can we have shellfish pots at her funeral? She wouldn't

have been able to eat them." The only person in the world whose dietary requirements you don't have to take into account at the funeral, and we're having this very serious discussion about whether it's the right thing to do.

I think it is so hard not to imbue the choices that you make for funeral food with the person and what they would have wanted. When, actually, the food at a funeral is probably a prop. It's a comfort, but not in the way we normally talk of comfort food. It gives people something to do with their hands. A platter of sandwiches gives people something to talk about if they can't talk about the elephant in the room.

AK: *Do you think there is a common thread in the kind of food served at funerals across cultures?*

OP: Food is never going to be what people are thinking about. I don't know a huge amount about other cultures' funeral food so I don't want to step on any toes, but I think it has to be something that doesn't dominate. Finger food, because people are standing up and talking. You don't want anything too whizzy. You're not going to have a celebration cake. If you have cake, it's in slices on a platter.

AK: *What was so comforting about that banana cake on the train after the funeral?* **OP:** Banana cake is perfect for grieving. Bananas have potassium, which is good for energy levels. It's got sugar, which we have been bred to find comforting since breast milk is sweeter than normal milk. We find succor and solace in sweet things. As much as I like a finger sandwich, cake

is innately more comforting. And it's stodge. It felt, sitting on a long train from Newcastle to London, like something that fills you. It has got what you need when you're grieving, particularly if you've been struggling to eat beforehand.

AK: *What would you want to have served at your funeral?* **OP:** I would have to have cake. I've turned my life into cake. But I certainly wouldn't want a big silly celebration cake. I would want really delicious loaf cake that's been cut into pieces for people to pick up. I think I'd want fizz. Some nod to celebration, even if it's a sad time. And buckets of tea, because that's what I like to drink. Really simple sandwiches, and sausage rolls because they are my favorite. That's how I'd like to be remembered: in a sausage roll.

ONE STEP FORWARD

by Pip Usher

When British researchers adorned a flight of stairs in a shopping mall with the instruction "Take the Stairs," it turned out that shoppers actually did. Over the course of three weeks, the number of people who chose to take the stairs increased by 190%, despite an escalator nearby. What gives? On a rational level, we know that exercise is beneficial. But our decision-making tends to be a chaotic process guided by intuition, unconscious bias and time pressures. On top of that, an estimated 80% of human behavior is automatic, with bad habits quickly becoming ingrained and remaining unchallenged. It turns out it's surprisingly easy to modify our aversion to energy-consuming stairs using mere suggestion. Put a staircase front and center (in most modern buildings it's the elevator that occupies prime position) and people will use it. Decorate stairwells, play music on them and ensure they benefit from natural light and people will be more likely to make healthy choices. These interventions force people out of autopilot and into conscious thought. Once there, the hope is that they will make a choice based on their best interests. A flight of stairs may not solve every woe wrought by office living, but it's certainly a step toward better health.
Photograph by Ingrid Fetell Lee

Carl Jan Cruz

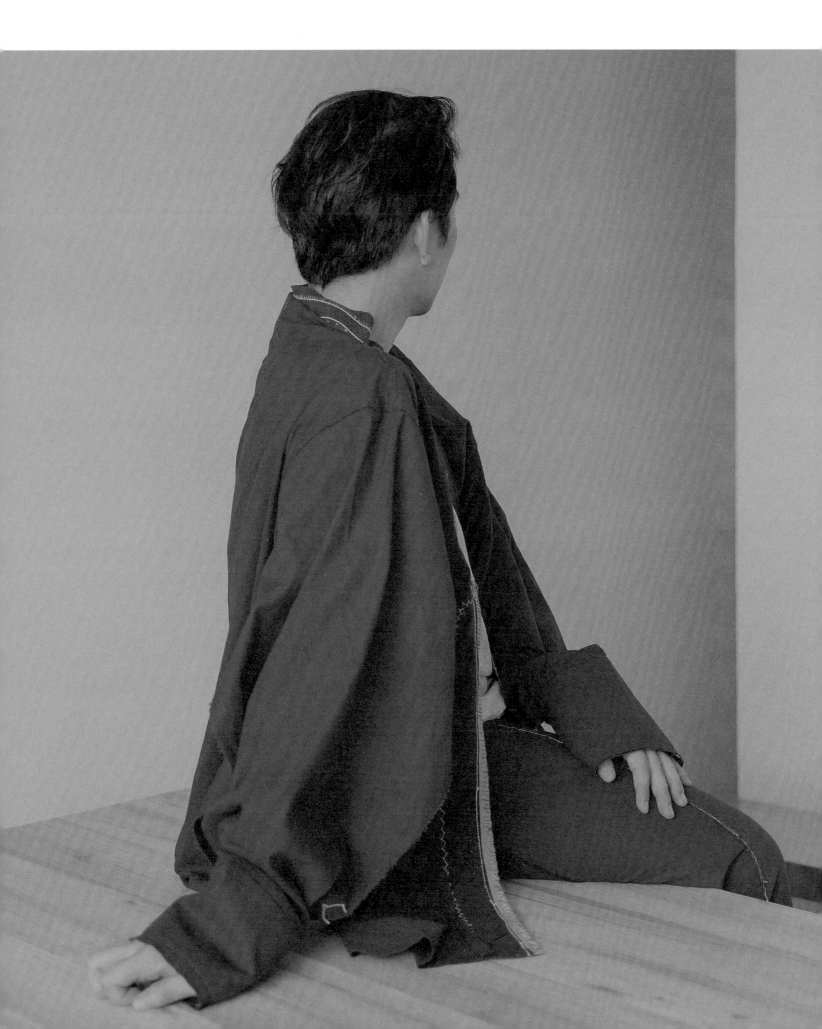

Before founding his namesake label in 2015, Carl Jan Cruz had followed the conventional trajectory of the fashion design student; he studied at London College of Fashion and then cut his teeth interning at Celine during the iconic reign of Phoebe Philo. Upon graduation, however, Cruz decided that he wanted to go back to his native Philippines and create his brand in the capital, Manila—a city not known for its fashion scene. It was also across the world from everyone and everything he thought he needed to build a thriving fashion label on the global stage.

NH: *What made you gravitate toward fashion as a student?* **CJC:** I grew up in three different places— Manila, Albay [a province in the Philippines] and London. I was living out of a suitcase, constantly packing and having limited options to wear. When you're young, you have those favorite things that you always want to wear so I'd have to find ways to create the outfits that I wanted. How I perceived clothes grew from a point of practicality, and my aesthetic was shaped through that.

NH: *What was the biggest challenge you encountered when setting up your brand?* **CJC:** Distance. Being halfway around the world is a literal act of meeting people halfway. It's been a constant challenge,

always prompting us to rethink how we can introduce ourselves to our audience. Doing our independent showroom in Paris twice a year and actually being able to communicate our work through the clothes is a vital way to bridge this. It doesn't take much to get someone to engage in something, so long as what you do is impactful. Though mostly posing a challenge, distance has helped us to realize the codes and processes of the brand.

NH: *Tell us about somaesthetics and how it plays a role in your work.* **CJC:** Somaesthetics is about considering yourself from a third-person perspective and confronting that viewpoint—an unbiased opinion about yourself. Somesthetics was a key principle in my final collection at London College of Fashion. I wanted to examine the uniqueness of how we grow up as individuals and apply this to something aesthetically. In the beginning, it was rooted in photographs and clothes that I'd collected over the years, but it became a search for something within the world of academia. It then shaped how the brand could take form and pushed me to not only create things that I liked but that actually represented a strong part of myself. Somesthetics is a big part of our DNA at the brand.

NH: *How would you describe the*

fashion scene in Manila? **CJC:** I think there is a healthy curiosity towards diversifying fashion, and how one can design and produce clothing within a contemporary sphere in the Philippines. I'd never have thought that a substantial part of our market share would be actual Filipino people who gravitate towards our ethos, but that's the case today and has been for four years running.

NH: *To what extent do the sociopolitical and economic circumstances of the Philippines impact your approach toward business or fashion?* **CJC:** Making peace with the idea that not everything in the Philippines would work in my favor— be it political, social or economic—was something that I had to do quite quickly. However, I sincerely believe that there is a possibility of being able to change things for the better. It's an interesting time in the Philippines in terms of its economy, politics and even religion. It prompts you to question your heritage and what you do. "Island time" is a useful factor too. Time is nearly always on your side here and the task is yours to figure out a way of dealing with it. A lifetime doesn't last forever so, for me, it's very much about being conscious of how my actions contribute not only to my own life but to the people and society around me.

In 2018, Cruz began collaborating with British artist and close friend Jessica Tremaine on "Pambahay Sculptures"—a series of homeware and objects blending ceramics and textiles.

RHIAN SASSEEN

Unbreak the Internet

A guide to being good online.

There's a cartoon that has become something of a meme since it was first published in 2008 in the American webcomic *xkcd*. In it, a stick figure sits hunched over a desktop computer, typing furiously. A voice off-panel asks, "Are you coming to bed?"

"I can't," the stick figure replies. "This is important... someone is wrong on the internet."

What exactly fuels our compulsive need to comment? Current events, local gossip, pop culture moments—it doesn't matter. Open up Twitter and you'll find a dense thicket of other people's opinions. Sometimes, this constant stream can be frightening. Other times, it can be fun, smart, even life-affirming—say, the outpouring of love one witnesses during a global sporting event. Or, equally fun: the outpouring of snark when a public figure behaves poorly.

It's a very human need that drives our impulse: We want to be acknowledged. Back in the golden days of print, letters to the editor—those corrections and comments so often mailed in by the bored, the elderly and the otherwise indisposed—were a pre-digital way for people to have their voices heard. The advent of the internet moved this online. There's a desire for community and belonging behind online comments; even those with the smallest followings on social media want to find their tribe and contribute to the world at large.

In recent years, a number of news sites, *Vice* and *NPR* among them, have closed commenting sections due to an increase in hate speech and trolling. Psychologists cite deindividuation—aka mob rule—as being at the root of trolling. Once deindividuation occurs, it's an easy next step to turning a commenter with an opposing viewpoint into just another "other," to be dehumanized and silenced at will. Digital spaces, after all, too often recreate the power dynamics of the physical world and perpetuate their same inequalities.

How can we safeguard against and combat this impulse? To comment most effectively online, individual commenters and communities might best be served by borrowing techniques from real-life protest movements and fighting back. If individuals join together in an act of community-minded solidarity—and what are so many online threads and conversations if not a form of digital consciousness raising?—then trolling can effectively be combated. Boycott platforms that allow and encourage trolling. Calling it out for what it is—hate speech—won't censor debate; it will allow debate to flourish, instead. Just as feminist groups in the 1980s banded together to "take back the night," it's time for all us to work together now to take back the internet.

Godwin's Law states that the longer an online discussion goes on, the more likely it is that someone will use a Nazi analogy.

Pretty Ugly

On the odd hierarchy of imperfections.

Left Photograph: David Smart, Right Photographs: Courtesy of Helle Mardahl and Talbot & Yoon

In the 1970s, the Japanese roboticist Masahiro Mori introduced the concept of the "uncanny valley." The valley effect occurs, he believed, when an artificial form is almost—but not quite—authentic enough to feel like the reality it is emulating. People experience an unpleasant disconnect when viewing such objects, and they become fearful and repelled. Technical perfection adds to, rather than subtracts from, the feeling; a perfect robotic face can leave the viewer disquieted and nauseated. Imperfections are sometimes added to mitigate the effect.

In real life, imperfections may be what we prize most dearly in those we find beautiful. They are not merely tolerated as necessary but celebrated and fantasized about in themselves. Flaws give us a chink through which to view great beauty without being overwhelmed—they make it safer to go on looking. Susan Sontag wrote in her 1975 essay *Fascinating Fascism*, "Painters and sculptors under the Nazis often depicted the nude, but they were forbidden to show any bodily imperfections. Their nudes look like pictures in physique magazines: pinups which are both sanctimoniously asexual and (in a technical sense) pornographic, for they have the perfection of a fantasy." Perfection is, in a sense, the opposite of life, suggesting as it does stasis and finality and the absence of variation.

The creation of art is meaningless if it aspires only to perfection in rendering. Art critic and essayist John Berger spoke of drawing and all creativity as the constant correction of errors, and if one were to arrive at a point where there were no errors left to correct, the work of art would probably be a very bad one. The poet Robert Lowell wrote, "… imperfection is the language of art./ Even the best writer in his best lines/ is incurably imperfect, crying for truth, knowledge/ honesty, inspiration he cannot have." The act of making art is not about gloating over what we have attained, but an appeal outward to that which we continue to seek. Like the beauty of a face we admire, imperfection in a work of art reveals the mystery of its creation. It is endlessly compelling, in a way that flawlessness can never be.

IN PRAISE OF BLOBS
by Pip Usher

In a world of sharp edges, the blobject —an amorphous object characterized by its soft, fluid form—offers a comforting alternative. Published in 2005, Steven Skov Holt and Mara Holt Skov's book, *Blobjects & Beyond: The New Fluidity in Design*, traces the emergence of the blobject in the late '90s, when digital software allowed these non-shapes to proliferate (think of the colorful curves of the original Apple iMac). Blobs have become synonymous with a friendlier face of product design. While critics may complain that such cuteness is childish, Holt Skov explains that "They offer an innate sense of optimism and hope." (Top: Goober by Talbot & Yoon. Center: Curly Kirbies by Talbot & Yoon. Bottom: Bon Bon Medi by Helle Mardahl.)

Behind great art, great bottoms.

Photograph: Jorge Perez Ortiz

CHARLES SHAFAIEH

Work All Angles

In James Joyce's *Ulysses*, the protagonist, Bloom, visits the National Museum of Ireland in Dublin. When viewing Greek sculptures, he feels compelled to look at the back of these statues, curious to know if they display anuses.

While we can justly bemoan how smartphones, computers and other screens have contributed to flattening our lived experience of the world, flatness has long been associated with how we experience art. Though this is inevitable when engaging with paintings and photographs, almost all objects in museums and galleries are kept behind glass, cordoned off or placed in such a way so that we can only see them on a single plane and from limited vantage points.

Bernini's sculpture *Apollo and Daphne* was never intended as an exception to this convention as it was originally placed in the corner of a room, but it realizes its dramatic potential now that it can be seen in the round at Rome's Galleria Borghese. Like the passage that inspired it from Ovid's *Metamorphoses*, in which a young maiden turns into a tree while the gods pursue her, the 17th-century marble sculpture, though static, conveys a narrative rather than a snapshot. Apollo's drapery appears in motion and Daphne's transformation an ongoing process, the complexity of which only reveals itself when the viewer moves around the work. The pair's facial expressions become more ambiguous, too, as different lenses on the story slowly reveal; at times their interaction seems predatory, at other times, tragic. Surprises such as these occur through movement, which introduces time as a dimension of art. This holds with abstract works as well, such as Richard Serra's monumental, folded-steel sculptures, like *Band*, which can stretch over 70 feet long and 12 feet high. "If you walk around a curve, you don't know how it's going to round," Serra observes. "It seems continuous and never-ending." Photos fail to convey this mysterious aspect of Serra's work, which demands full-body engagement.

A shift in the power dynamic between art and observer occurs in pieces viewed in the round, as the latter can no longer claim control. The same principle exists with theater performed in the round, which creates the opportunity for more equal and direct confrontations between audience and actor than those that occur when using a proscenium stage. Work kept at a distance and which can be consumed in a glance allows one to maintain a sense of control. But, as with those walking around Serra's sculptures, spectators cannot be passive in the round. Rather, they must give up their dominant stance, enter into a dialogue and risk being unsettled.

At 30 years old, Riley Harper has already accrued almost a quarter century of experience as a stuntman. It was the family trade, and his dad got him his first job on set (falling down some stairs) when he was six. Since then, he's spent the majority of his working life crashing cars, being set on fire and taking punches on behalf of Hollywood's most recognizable faces. He talks to *Bella Gladman* about the serious work behind being a professional daredevil.

BG: *Are you a tough guy?* **RH:** It depends how you look at "tough guy." I was raised racing motorcycles, breaking bones and getting concussions—dealing with pain at a young age. But the mindset's the tough part. The funniest thing people say when they hear what I do is, "I can do that, I'm crazy." That's the opposite of what you have to be. Don't get me wrong, you have to be a little crazy. But you also have to be calculated.

BG: *How do you balance wanting to control things on set and just "going with it"?* **RH:** You can prepare as much as possible, but when it comes down to it, you have to

perform. The cameras turn on, and there are 100 people standing and watching. TV world is very fast-moving compared to movies—there's no time to rehearse. You arrive, everything's already set up, and you have to slide a car at 40 miles an hour, next to a camera with a camera operator on it. That's nerve-racking. You're just flying by the seat of your pants.

BG: *Do you think about danger in a more long-term capacity?* **RH:** I always try to have a good chunk of money saved up so I know I'm good for six months. The potential of getting hurt's always there. If it wasn't, it wouldn't be so appealing. Knowing you can get hurt makes you operate differently—your instincts come into play.

BG: *What has being a stuntman taught you about fear?* **RH:** How to categorize it. There are so many different types: fear of being embarrassed, hurt, or of losing. Once you categorize it, you can accept it. Fear can make you do some amazing things, but it can stop you doing them too. It's being able to forget about the fear and go do whatever it is that scares you. The outcome's usually pretty awesome.

Harper started racing motocross at the age of four. At 18, he booked a major gig on the blockbuster *Wanted*, driving with Angelina Jolie harnessed to the hood of a car. Photograph: Trevor King

BELLA GLADMAN

Riley Harper

The California stuntman on feeling the fear, and doing it anyway.

BEN SHATTUCK

The Road Not Taken

On sliding doors and greener grass.

Your introduction to the famous Robert Frost poem "The Road Not Taken" might have been when your grade-school teacher told you that the road in question was the one fewer people traveled. The road of independence. The better road. Go the wilder route, the poem says. Bushwhack to unseen beauty! Discover what others haven't.

You may have held on to that interpretation, but the road not taken, if you read carefully, is clearly not the same road as the "one less traveled." The road not taken is simply the other road— the one that "bent in the undergrowth" of the yellow wood. The roads aren't even that different, as described in these overlooked lines: "Though as for that the passing there/ Had worn them really about the same,/ And both that morning equally lay/ In leaves no step had trodden black."

The poem is an anxiously pensive narrative of what-ifs, about blaming misfortune on decisions made long ago. You see the truth in the poem as you enter adulthood, experiencing firsthand how small choices lead to big changes. If only I'd taken that other job, you think, I'd be happier. If only I'd followed my lover to Paris, gone to a different college, taken that semester abroad. Unhappiness is mother to regret, and regret mother to blame.

Not being able to reverse your decisions stings: "Yet knowing how way leads on to way," Frost wrote of the forked road, "I doubted if I should ever come back."

The "if-I'd-only" moments increase with age, as you find yourself in a landscape of friends, work and a relationship shaped by a chain of decisions. Through the years, you see how the branches of your ghost lives would have split and grown and split, and you might one day, when you're feeling particularly unhappy, throw your head back to marvel at the tree of intersections, each twig tipped with the leaf of a different life. In your less anxious moments, you'd see the poem as consolation: No matter the chosen path, we all, even the great Robert Frost, wonder where the other road led. "I shall be telling this with a sigh," the narrator laments before saying he took the road "less traveled by."

It becomes easy to see how misfortune can be whittled down to a logic of wrong paths that led to missed opportunities. Among the most famous: Western Union rejecting Alexander Graham Bell's telephone patent offer, calling the device "idiotic." Hewlett-Packard telling Steve Wozniak they weren't interested in his personal computer idea. Every one of the 15 publishing houses that rejected J.K.

Rowling's wizard books. It could seem that all misfortune could be avoided—and fortune gained—if only the right path was taken.

But you might do well to crack open a biography on Frost. *The Letters of Robert Frost* includes a missive from Frost to his hiking partner, Edward Thomas, in which he admitted he was frustrated when his new poem, "The Road Not Taken," was taken seriously at a college reading in 1915. "Despite," Frost wrote, "doing my best to make it obvious by my manner that I was fooling."

The poem was a joke meant for Thomas, who, Frost noticed, spent his time in the English countryside bemoaning what they might have seen had they taken another path. The poem is a critique of wondering about what might have been, not a sober review of opportunity cost. Regret is injurious, Frost intended to say. By spending your walk staring at the ground, grumbling about the road not taken, you missed the birdsong and honeysuckle and sunlight sifting through the yellow canopy. The path you've taken is the always right one, Frost meant, because it's also always the wrong one. Happiness comes from walking the path, feeling the ground. So buck up, and just enjoy the damn view.

In the 1998 rom-com *Sliding Doors*, the protagonist's life plays out on two very different tracks according to whether she catches a train (and finds her partner cheating) or misses it (and doesn't).

RIMA SABINA AOUF

How to Read the News

To wise up, slow down.

"Reading the morning newspaper is the realist's morning prayer," wrote the philosopher Hegel at the turn of the 1800s. It was a time when the mass dissemination of news was allowing people to make decisions based on something concrete, beyond religious beliefs.

Would Hegel have seen the sanctity in propping yourself up on one elbow half-conscious in bed to scroll through Twitter? Certainly, the contemporary reality of nonstop news is one he never could have predicted. The average adult in the US now spends more than 11 hours per day listening to, watching, reading or otherwise interacting with some sort of media. A good part of this is news—news that comes tumbling into our brain throughout the day via our social media feeds. It's so constant that many of us report feeling anxious or overwhelmed by the very task of reading it.

And it raises the question: If it was essential to seek out the news to be a good citizen in a time of information scarcity, is it now essential to limit or modulate your news intake to be a good citizen living in an era of information overload?

That's one of the arguments behind "slow journalism." Similar to other "slow" movements such as "slow food" and "slow fashion," slow journalism encourages the conscious and ethical consumption of a quality product. An example is UK-based magazine *Delayed Gratification*, which makes a point of covering stories in longform that have been out of the headlines for three months. The magazine's founder, Rob Orchard, told *Kinfolk* that he thinks we've reached a "new normal" of news-reading typified by a "constant, low-level anxiety" and "knee-jerk reactions." He says, "The reason that people are reporting that feeling of information overload is because they are anxious, and they should be anxious because we're putting our brains through something that no generation of humans has ever put themselves through before—and we're doing it willingly."

Orchard has a few recommendations for people wanting to take control of their news diet and read less but better. The first two tips: Pay for your news, and ensure you have a basic understanding of the industry and ecosystem that exists behind it. "If you enjoy living in a democracy, where corruption and power are held to account, then you need to be part of the group that funds that holding to account," says Orchard.

His steps are all about being a conscious consumer, controlling both your inputs and feedback into the system. But there's another sense in which control relates to our experience of reading news: The news makes us realize how very little control we have. For some of us, there are few greater anxiety triggers. Mass shootings, border detention, global environmental catastrophe—we get little more than one chance every few years to influence the outcomes of these events when we vote in elections. But what if there was a way to filter for the news we *can* control? Arguably, there is, and it's called local news. That's not just what's happening at town hall but also what's going on at community gardens, migrant welcome committees, environmental action groups—forums we can very much affect. To engage with these institutions isn't to turn our backs on the great injustices of the world. Far from it: In his manifesto, *Out of the Wreckage*, British writer George Monbiot argues that without the strong workforce of previous years, it makes sense for local communities to be the organizing base of a positive big-picture political movement, "formed around participatory culture, building outwards to revive national and global politics."

Unfortunately, local news isn't abundant. Small newsrooms have been decimated more than those at any other level by economic changes. In fact, when Facebook started its locally focused news feed earlier in 2019, it found that nearly half of Americans lived in "news deserts": There weren't enough original local stories to implement the service. (That Facebook's algorithm had previously deprioritized them to death is, of course, a bitter irony.)

So try substituting a local paper or site for one of your global news sources each week. But do so with Orchard's words in mind and consider how we might act on the information we receive.

Hans Rosling coined the idea of "factfulness" as a way of contextualizing world news: focus on the big picture rather than every sad story and you'll see that many aspects of life are improving.

"We're putting our brains through something that no generation of humans has ever put themselves through before."

The meaning of metaphors.

TIM HORNYAK

Picture This

In *On Writing*, horror author Stephen King praised metaphors for making it possible to "see an old thing in a new and vivid way."

As a child, I read somewhere that God gave humanity metaphor to help us better understand the world. But we don't need religion to see that the more complex or powerful a sensation, the more words fail us. That's why we use comparisons: Simile and metaphor can be far more effective than mere adjectives in communicating what we feel. When we evoke a familiar sensation, our listeners and readers can grasp that meaning instantly. Similes begin with "like" or "as" and offer a direct comparison with something: As busy as a bee. Metaphors go further, equating one thing with another: "All the world's a stage," Jaques tells us in Shakespeare's *As You Like It*. Derived from the Greek *metaphorá*, meaning to transfer, metaphors yoke separate concepts. In the *Poetics*, Aristotle wrote that using them well can be a mark of genius.

Metaphors are embedded in everyday language ("time is money"), perhaps because they have a neurological basis. Cognitive linguist George Lakoff has described how, from an early age, our brains learn to associate sensations— warmth and affection, for example—forming neural circuits between brain regions involved. By the time we're six or seven, we've learned hundreds of such physical associations. Neuroscientist Vicky Lai and colleagues recently found that when people hear a phrase such as "bend the rules," the brain areas that process tactile sensations, such as the action of bending, activate immediately.

We're hardwired for metaphor, and we're naturals at perceiving similarities in disparate things. Heraclitus saw the same essence in the flow of a river and the passage of time. That insight not only gives us the metaphorical "time is a river," it opens the door to abstract thinking. Metaphors are particularly handy when talking about things that aren't physically present. The Bible overflows with poetic expressions such as "The Lord is my shepherd; I shall not want." And Einstein—whose own name is now a metaphor for "genius"—used allegorical moving trains, beams of light and twins in rockets in his thought experiments to explain the nature of spacetime. Thinking metaphorically, then, is not only what our brains have evolved to do automatically over time, but it also represents our loftiest expressions in art, philosophy and spirituality. We are Homo metaphoricus.

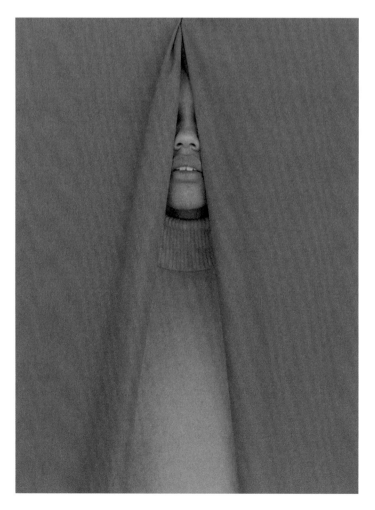

Photograph: Brooke DiDonato / Agence VU

Left Photographs: Courtesy of Ferm Living, Christian Møller Andersen and WallpaperSTORE*. Right Photograph: Iringó Demeter

CALL ME BABY

by Pip Usher

If you have a proclivity for calling your partner pet names, blame your mother. According to research, it's a habit acquired as an infant while listening to that first love—your materfamilias—coo endearments. Years later, such bonding techniques resurface in romantic relationships in the form of affectionate nicknames. While they may induce eye rolls and faux gagging from others, don't throw the baby names out with the bathwater just yet. All those "sweethearts" and "darlings" signify a relationship that's going strong, with research showing a correlation between a couples' happiness and the number of endearments they use. (Top: Gift Tags by Ferm Living. Center: Brass Card Holders by Horn Please. Bottom: Luggage Tag by Ettinger.)

Word: Daddy

When did a sweet word get so spicy?

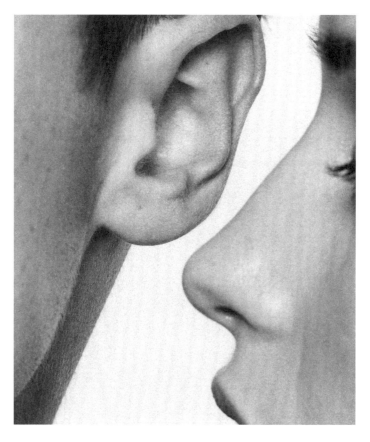

Etymology: The word "daddy" has been on an adventure ever since it moved beyond the purely paternal in the 1920s. Starting, according to the Oxford English Dictionary, as a word "most commonly used in children's language," "daddy" has become a term of endearment when used between adults in non-familial or sexually intimate relationships. These relationships tend to be ones with potent power dynamics, commonly involving submission to masculine authority.

The internet has toyed with the term and subverted it. Twitter is awash with people addressing the likes of Barack Obama, Drake and Dwayne "The Rock" Johnson as "daddy." Bernie Sanders is also not immune.

What constitutes a "daddy" is mercurial. Daddies don't *have* to be old. According to Mike Albo writing in *The Cut*, in the gay community, where "daddy" reportedly took off as part of the leather subculture, it has more to do with aesthetics: "facial hair and meat on his bones." Look to spring chicken Zayn Malik, commonly referred to as "daddy," for evidence—as well as

the character of Dominga "Daddy" Duarte in *Orange Is the New Black* for proof that gender isn't a prerequisite, either.

For Eve Peyser, writing in *New York* magazine: "What differentiates today's iteration of daddy [as used by heterosexual millennial women] from past conceptions is we're having way more fun with it."

Meaning: Linguists hold that baby talk can be a valuable—if cloying—form of couples bonding. According to Frank Nuessel, interviewed by *Vice*, baby talk "is about providing adults with a space to express themselves, free of the stultifying conventions of normal human conversation." Calling someone you are sexually attracted to "daddy" certainly falls outside the usual patter.

When "daddy" is specifically used to denote female submission to masculinity, the gender politics are knotty, but Peyser writes that using "daddy" can be empowering. By claiming it as their own women, are, she says, gently mocking "the patriarchal structures we're playing into." See the "daddy" tweets sometimes sent to the pope for reference.

Copenhagen's queen of color makes the case for "weird" shades and dark rooms.

JAMES CLASPER

Josephine Akvama Hoffmeyer

Josephine Akvama Hoffmeyer is an equal opportunity designer. "There's no such thing as an ugly color, a bad color or a beautiful color. And I don't have a favorite color," says the creative director of File Under Pop, the Copenhagen-based design studio she founded in 2015. Its name is a nod to Hoffmeyer's past: A former professional singer, she once performed backing vocals for Joe Cocker and Rick Astley. Equally fitting, the 64 colors in File Under Pop's paint collection take their names from popular songs (Think: Raspberry Beret, Pale Blue Eyes and Purple Haze). Along with hand-painted wallpaper and tiles handcrafted from Sicilian lava stone, File Under Pop's paints comprise the "bag of tools" that Hoffmeyer uses to transform spaces for top-drawer clients such as Hermès and Mikkeller.

JC: *Why are you drawn to working with colors?* **JAH:** Because of the emotional tensions and the harmony or disharmony that you can create with them.

JC: *Harmony's an interesting choice of word.* **JAH:** Well, I love music and I used to sing and write music. Music is all about chords, notes, harmony and tension. They are all the ingredients you use to make music, and I use them in my work today.

JC: *In terms of combining colors?* **JAH:** Yes, but also combining tiles and colors. When you're creating a space, you need to weigh how much tension to give one object compared to another. Right now we're sitting in a room with three different shades of green, and I've used this weird little yellow—it's called Sahara Sand—to spice it up. It's like music, how you use different instruments. Like maybe you want horns to say this or a guitar to say that at an important moment in the song. When you talk about color, it's important to discuss texture and the material you're working on or around. The object, its shape, the material—it all works together with the color, and that's how it gets to be super-sensual or extremely powerful, or whatever it is you want to express. Look at the wooden panel above the door. It's got a matte finish that makes it look edible—like the glazing on a cake.

JC: *Do you have any rules when it comes to colors? Are there any that you would never use on, say, the ceiling?* **JAH:** No—it depends on the sum of everything. It depends on how the light gets in, whether the room is facing north or south, whether there's a lot of furniture, and so on. It's also a question of how you're going to live in that space and what function you're

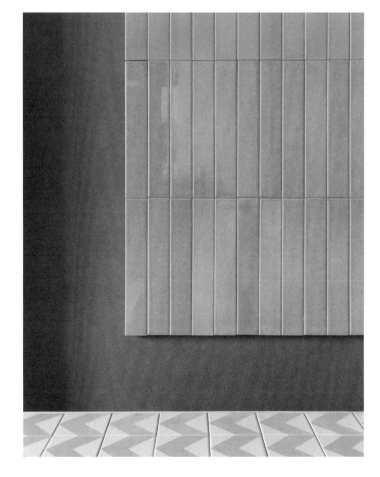

looking for. For example, I love to sleep in a very dark, warm color in my summerhouse, because when I go there, I want to be quiet. I don't want to do too many things. I want to have my slow life.

JC: *How do you describe yourself?* JAH: I'm very curious and I'm also brave, because I don't mind going all the way to the edge of things. I trust that everything will fall into place. That's quite important for my work. I never graduated [from Parsons School of Design in New York City], so in a way, I'm an autodidact. I developed a strong sense of creative intuition, which gives me a lot of freedom not to be too dedicated to a certain code or scheme for how to do things.

JC: *Do you often challenge your clients to be braver too?* JAH: Some are afraid of colors because they've seen them up against white panels and white ceilings, which the colors stand out against. So you have to push and challenge them. They'll say, "We have a very dark bathroom, absolutely no daylight gets in, so we need to find a very light color for it." I think it's better—or at least I try—to say, "Why? You're not going to be in there long and you can always work with the lighting. And isn't it beautiful to go with the darkness?" Most of the time I succeed in getting people to think about what could be done differently to what they expected. Because what we expect is

often what we've seen or what other people tell us.

JC: *Tell me about your studio and where it's located.* JAH: We're in a beautiful, historic part of Copenhagen. The queen lives nearby, there are beautiful parks and museums, and the seafront is right here. Every day I go into our big meeting room, which has these huge windows, and looks out at the Marble Church, where it says, "Life, Truth and Jesus." I'm not really religious, but it's a good way of connecting with something bigger than myself, with some kind of universal force.

JC: *What else do you draw inspiration from?* JAH: Nature. I walk a lot, I go winter bathing and I have a summerhouse where I go to connect with nature and be completely still and silent. I'm also inspired by art exhibitions and by traveling.

JC: *Copenhagen is renowned for its astonishing light, which must also inspire you.* JAH: That's true. I love to work with matte finishes. In fact, our paint has 1% of shine, which maintains and holds the light from outside—daylight—in a beautiful and honest way. The most important thing in the world for me is honesty. Honesty is 80% of beauty, if you want to define what beauty is. If you have a very shiny surface, it will reflect light and not be as honest. Matte finishes stay as close to the reality of your true experience of the

light as possible. Most paint producers today try to make their colors as stable and as even as possible. They want their colors to look more or less the same from nine in the morning until five in the evening. I like the fact that colors are alive, that they can change and that they can work together with the light.

JC: *The stereotypical Scandinavian look is monochromatic—lots of whites, grays and blacks—yet there was much more vibrant use of color in Denmark around the midcentury. What happened to the Danish love for colors?* JAH: First of all, I think everything that once was still is. It may be that it's hidden or just not as obvious. But it never went away. Second, people in Denmark are much more vibrant and much more outgoing than I remember from my childhood. I do think there's a new awareness of how we connect with and interact with colors.

JC: *How much does the Scandinavian sensibility influence you?* JAH: It's relevant and important to me. I find the Scandinavian mood very simple and quite honest, in a broad sense. We're very down-to-earth people. So that simplicity and coolness is half of me, but I also have African roots, from my father—from Ghana. So I have some craziness, some wildness, and I try to make the two sides meet.

Last year, Hoffmeyer teamed up with Italian designer Elisa Ossino to rent an apartment in Milan which the duo uses as a livable showcase for their design studio, H+O.

2
Features

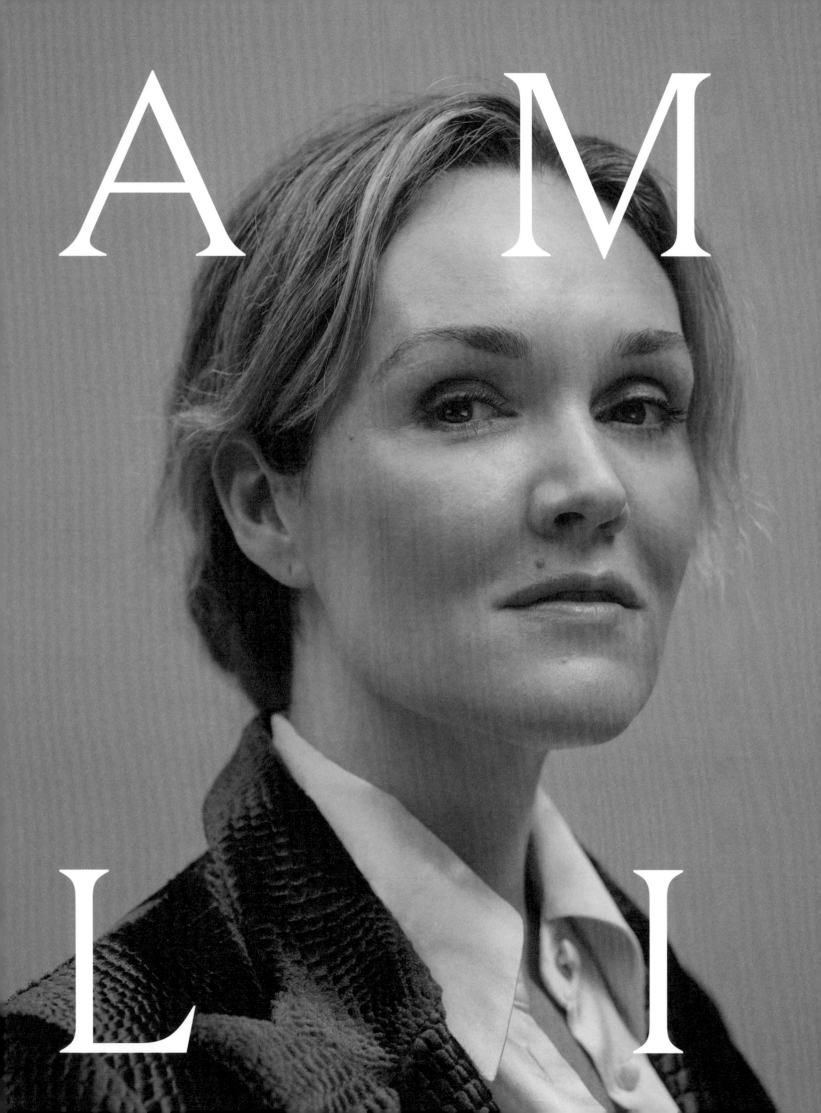

A
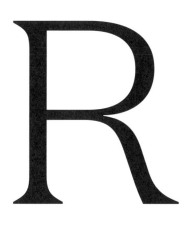
R

Y
L

S

What happens when a precociously talented
undercover CIA officer turns her mind to peace? *Amaryllis Fox*
talks to *Robert Ito* about her life less ordinary.

Photography by
Emman Montalvan

Styling by
Jardine Hammond

Amaryllis Fox was a student at Georgetown when she developed an algorithm to identify likely terrorist safe havens. The CIA recruited her when she was 22, and she spent the next decade going deeper and deeper undercover in the world's most dangerous places. What she learned there changed the way she thought about conflict and communication for good.

In 2009, Amaryllis Fox flew to Pakistan in the hopes of convincing representatives from three extremist groups not to detonate a bomb in the middle of a crowded city center there. Here's a community center you would hit, she told them, pointing at a spot on a tourist map. Here are two schools. Here is a mosque. Innocents would die, she told the men, all of whom had ties to Al Qaeda and the Taliban. Americans would die, yes, but so would Muslims, in even greater numbers. Fox appealed to them as men of honor, as men of God. Do not do this thing, she told them.

Before this fateful meeting in a cramped, book-filled apartment in Karachi, Fox had already spent much of the past decade as an undercover officer in the CIA. Over the years she had tracked the flow of weapons of mass destruction from the agency's counterterrorism center in Iraq, infiltrated terrorist groups in Southeast Asia and the Middle East and negotiated with arms dealers who were selling chemical and biological weapons on the global black market. As a Clandestine Service officer, one of her primary jobs was meeting with people who wanted to do grave harm to others, either by committing acts of terrorism themselves or by supplying arms and aid.

For most of her time in the agency, few outsiders knew just what Fox was doing or where she was doing it: not her closest friends nor her first husband, not her mother or father, not her older brother, Ben, nor her younger sister, Antonia. During much of her time in the field, they thought she was an intrepid art dealer, buying and selling indigenous art for wealthy collectors. Even many of her closest colleagues in the CIA were kept in the dark about her missions and whereabouts.

Since leaving the CIA, however, Fox has undergone what appears to be, at first blush, the unlikeliest of transformations. After years spent in a shadow world living among people intent on making war, she has come out, boldly—exuberantly even—as one of the country's most visible and outspoken advocates for peace. In a three-minute video produced in 2016 that quickly went viral, Fox pleads her case. "If I learned one lesson from my time with the CIA, it is this: Everybody believes they are the good guy," she begins. We need to listen to our enemies, she explains, to try to see them as they see themselves, and vice versa. Consider this: If US forces were in a Hollywood sci-fi flick, would audiences be cheering for *them*? "To the rest of the world," an Al Qaeda fighter once told her, "you are the Empire, and we are Luke and Han."

"This is how the kung fu masters work, right? If a force hits you, you can own it."

On a recent afternoon, Fox was at the San Vicente Bungalows in West Hollywood, a members-only club midway between Melrose Avenue and the Sunset Strip. Before I'm allowed to meet her, a desk attendant asks for my cellphone, ever so politely, and places tiny stickers emblazoned with palm trees and the club's name over the camera lenses. It's standard policy at the paparazzi-free zone, but seems almost absurdly low-tech under the circumstances, given the levels of care that Fox used to conceal her identity in her past life. For Fox, however, the stickers and all they represent aren't really why she comes here: She just likes the food and tea and outdoor setting, and the fact that it's close to a lot of her current hangouts, and not so far from her home.

Hello, hello, she says, signaling me over to her small table. She had spent the morning swimming in the Pacific, she tells me, and wonders if I'd like something to eat? Over lunch, she describes some of the myriad twists and turns that her life has taken, including how she came to be in the CIA, and how later, she came to leave it. Talk to her long enough, and two things become very clear. First, she likes to find common ground in everything and everyone, so, for instance, while she was in the CIA and I was not, we're both parents, and humans, and living in LA, which makes us almost kin, at least in the human family. Second, she feels things more deeply than most, and definitely deeper than is probably good for one's mental health.

"As a child, it was overwhelming," she says. "At times, seeing the suffering of the world felt as though it would drown me. It wasn't until I was at university and a friend of mine pointed out, this is how the kung fu masters work, right? If a force hits you, you can sort of own it and metabolize it and put it back out into the world, and it will fuel your work."

Fox was born Amaryllis Damerell Thornber in 1980. Her father became one of the youngest economics professors in the history of the University of Chicago; her mother, an actress and British national, grew up in a stately home in the English countryside. Raised as an Episcopalian, Fox dreamed of one day becoming a priest. As a child, she loved *The Velveteen Rabbit*, a tale about "the beauty of being real even if you're shabby and your eyes have been loved off," and the Paddington books. Her mother would read the stories to Fox and her brother and sister, acting out the parts as she went. C.S. Lewis' Narnia series, with its rich Christian allegory and tales of heroism and youthful camaraderie, was another favorite. "They did a really wonderful job of using adventure to introduce kids to a sense of responsibility and guardianship toward one another and toward the world," she says. "And there's the promise that, as long as you work and sacrifice, spring will follow winter."

A precocious student, Fox spent her days in high school learning Sanskrit and theoretical physics and falling in love with the writings of Henry David Thoreau. When it came time for her to select a university, she was faced with a difficult (albeit enviable) choice: the US Naval Academy, proving ground for generations of Navy and Marine Corps officers, or Oxford, alma mater of Stephen Hawking and Sir Walter Raleigh. Annapolis offered her the chance to became a naval aviator, the most direct path, she reasoned, to becoming a NASA shuttle pilot. "I wanted to be a Blue Angel and join the space program," she says. "It was really only the draw of the library at Oxford that made me think, well, I'll just do this one other application." The previous summer, Fox had completed the Naval Academy's "plebe summer," a program that simulates the hardships and hazing of that school's famously brutal first year, so Annapolis was already a lock. But then Oxford said yes, too. If she went to the Naval Academy, she'd study aerospace engineering; if she picked Oxford, she'd study theology and law. "It was a good problem to have," she admits.

In the end, Fox chose Oxford, but she decided to spend a gap year in Myanmar, where she lived and worked in a refugee camp on the border of Myanmar and Thailand. While there, she met rebel fighters and former political prisoners, and filmed a clandestine interview with Aung San Suu Kyi, the Myanmar leader and Nobel laureate who was, at the time, under house arrest. After smuggling the film out of the country inside her vagina, Fox took the recording, with Suu Kyi's rare and inspiring call to action, to the BBC and CNN. The next month, Fox was at Oxford, albeit in flip-flops and with a renewed sense of purpose.

For the next three years, Fox studied theology and international law, volunteered for Amnesty International, and made friends. In the September before her final year at Oxford, hijackers flew American Airlines Flight 11 into the North Tower of the World Trade Center. Four months later, Daniel Pearl, a reporter for *The Wall Street Journal* and a "writing hero" of Fox's, was kidnapped and beheaded by terrorists in Pakistan. Fox recalled how, more than a decade before, when she was in third grade, she had lost one of her best friends on Pan Am Flight 103, which was destroyed by a terrorist's bomb over Lockerbie, Scotland. Fox knew she had to do something, even if she wasn't sure quite what.

Hair/Makeup: Nicole Wittman, Photo Assistants: Fred Mitchell and Patrick Molina

That fall, after graduating from Oxford, she began a master's program in conflict and terrorism at Georgetown University in Washington, D.C. "For me, I came to my work in counterterrorism having really faced the cost of terrorism on a personal level," she says. "And having felt those losses so deeply as a young person, when I started in the world of counterterrorism, it really wasn't with the view to find some sort of common ground. It was very much about destroying the adversary and getting them off the chessboard."

While studying at Georgetown, Fox developed an algorithm to identify areas around the world most likely to be used as terrorist safe havens. The project caught the attention of a CIA officer-in-residence at the university, who recruited Fox in 2003. She was 22. For the next eight years, Fox lived the life of a CIA agent, eventually becoming a member of the agency's elite Clandestine Service. She worked on kidnapping cases as she planned her first wedding, and discovered how flaws on American watch lists were leading to the torture of innocent victims worldwide. In 2008, Fox gave birth to a daughter, Zoe.

Fox was supremely good at what she did, so good that each successive assignment led to another, more challenging and dangerous one. But even as her responsibilities rose within the agency, she began to question the CIA's tactics and its general approach to fighting terrorism. Should we be trying to convince our enemies that we could be just as fearsome as they? Or should we be identifying the areas where our humanity overlaps with theirs? After nearly a decade as an agent, Fox left the CIA in 2010. She came to California to stay with her mother and stepfather, and slowly went about the task of finding her true self, the one she had kept hidden behind assorted disguises. "It was a long arc," she admits. "But in the end, I learned that the authentic, vulnerable version of myself, with no cover and no sidearm and no protection of alias or fiction, is better equipped to do the work of peace in the world than the version of me that might have felt safe, but was locked away under all these things."

Back in the US, Fox sought out opportunities to use the skills she had learned in the CIA among people who weren't, say, arms dealers or terrorists. At California's Pelican Bay State Prison, the notorious former home of Charles Manson and Marion "Suge" Knight, she helped prisoners prepare to make amends to survivors of their crimes. In Los Angeles, she worked with gang members who were trying to reintegrate into their communities; in northern Iraq, she brought US and Iraqi veterans together to talk about their shared experiences during the wars. "I found that the skills I had learned to bring adversaries together in conversation are actually in great, dire demand in today's society," she says.

On July 7, 2018, Fox married Robert F. Kennedy III, scion of the Kennedy clan, at the family's compound in Hyannis Port, Massachusetts. The two live in Laurel Canyon in the Hollywood Hills with Zoe, now 11, and their seven-month-old daughter, Bobby, aka Bobcat. Zoe attends a socially progressive grade school with a strong music and arts program, fitting for an area that Jim Morrison, Joni Mitchell and the Mamas and the Papas once called home.

Left: Fox wears a sweater by Orseund Iris, a dress by Giuseppe di Morabito. Previous spread: She wears a sweater by Reiss and a ring by Sophie Buhai. Overleaf: Sheer trench coat by Toga, trousers by Equipment and shoes by Ego.

One of their favorite things to do is pack their kids into a 1962 school bus that they converted into an RV ("it has a little kitchen and a bedroom and a hanging crochet cradle for the baby"), and drive up to a national forest to camp and fish for trout. The weekend before I met Fox, she'd been "off the grid," doing just that. "We were in the redwoods," she says. "You can show up and put $20 on your honor in a slot to reserve your spot, and you have the most beautiful view in the world."

In October 2019, Knopf published Fox's memoir, *Life Undercover: Coming of Age in the CIA*. The book has all the twists and turns and exotic locales that one might expect from the spy thriller that it is, but it also goes deep into what it means to live the life of a CIA spook as a human being, and what sorts of strains that puts on one's loves and relationships and psyche. The story has already captured the attention of Hollywood, with the Academy Award-winning actress Brie Larson set to star in a new drama series based on Fox's life. "She is one of my favorite people to talk to about geopolitics," she says of Larson. "I find her extremely entertaining company." Fox also spent the last year working on a new Netflix documentary series "about the economics that drive the worldwide war on drugs, and why it'll never work."

These various projects have kept Fox from doing something she's wanted to do for years, even before she started work on her memoir: write a book for kids. Her lifelong love of children's literature probably has a lot to do with that, and *Life Undercover* ends with a nod to *The Velveteen Rabbit*, a book she first read to her daughter not long before leaving the CIA. The memoir also has references to the Harry Potter books, *Star Trek* and to the legendary Japanese animator Hayao Miyazaki. So is Fox, former CIA agent and current advocate for peace, a nerd? "I am very much a nerd," she says with a laugh. "I love science fiction. I love fantasy. I think there is a freedom that comes with telling stories about very difficult topics against fictional backgrounds." She's happy to discuss the themes of autocracy and torture and the struggle for purpose in J.K. Rowling's books, and to tell you about how fans of Hogwarts end up being, in a nutshell, better, more empathetic people. They've done studies on it, she says.

Fox is currently putting the finishing touches on her own YA book, which will be released in 2020. "We are shaped so much by the stories we internalize as young people," she says. "If you go back to the earliest human days sitting around the campfire, stories are really what allow us to have experiences beyond our own life, and to understand perspectives that are different from ours. And I think the habits we form around being open or not open to stories as children go with us for the rest of our lives."

Writing these books, she insists, is not altogether different from the work she did in the CIA. In both, she says, you're appealing to things that are common in all of us. Back in Pakistan, she was reaching out to the representatives of Al Qaeda as honorable men (in the end, the terrorist groups, thanks to Fox's appeals, did not bomb the city center). Today, in Los Angeles, she's trying to inspire people to reach out across the divisions that exist in their own communities. "I'm immensely proud of the work that I did at the CIA," she says. "And when I left, it was at a point where I had done the work that I was meant to do, and it was time to move on and speak to a different set of readers."

Fox believes that humans ultimately want to get along, despite what all the polls and political pundits might say. "I think, at our core, humans are hopeful," she says. "We yearn for connection. And if you're alive to the possibility of climbing inside the shoes of someone with whom you disagree, it can become a pretty exhilarating thing. Even if you'll never agree with them, even if their worldview seems so distant from yours, it allows you to better understand how to prevent conflict with that person and move forward, in a way, hopefully, that works for both of you."

"The skills I had learned to bring adversaries together in conversation are actually in great, dire demand in today's society."

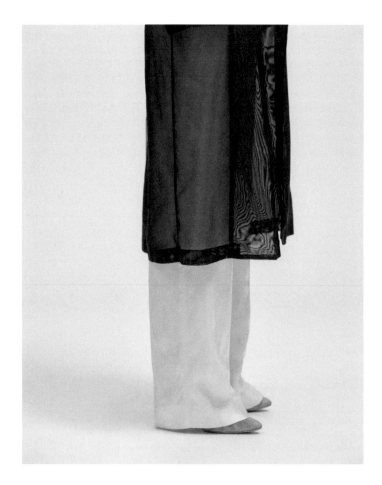

Day in the Life:
Mennlay Golokeh Aggrey

Meet the Mexico City-based "weed *tía*" who's balancing entrepreneurship with activism in her booming, inequitable industry. Words by *Scarlett Lindeman* & Photography by *Victoria Barmak*

"I often call myself, 'weed tía'. I want it to come from a place of comfort, of nurturing."

Every Tuesday, Pachuca Street in Colonia Condesa blossoms into a *tianguis*—one of Mexico City's colorful, temporary, open-air bazaars. I'm following Mennlay Golokeh Aggrey through the scrum—we're winding our way through vegetable vendors offering *huitlacoche* and neon-green fava beans, past stands of cell phone chargers and bootleg Blu-ray discs. "This is where I get some of my basic bitch office-worker button-downs," she chuckles, floating through a bottleneck of families and tourists.

We had arranged to meet at a new restaurant. I had double-checked the hours and their Instagram page, but we arrive to find it shuttered—plans in Mexico City are often stymied by unanticipated hiccups. This city and her work, as author, activist and cannabis cultivator, demand the flexibility and patience that Aggrey stores in leagues. "Tacos it is, then," she says, as we pivot to the outdoor market.

Aggrey is a veteran of the marijuana industry and has moved through a series of overlapping roles over the years: as a canna-

bis cultivator, user-advocate, writer and community leader. Much of our talk centers on the shifting nature (and many shades of legality) of an industry starting to regulate. Fifteen years ago, she was growing weed in Humboldt County, California, with a small, thriving grow-op in the two-car garage where she was living. She was growing in a way that was supposedly legal under the Compassionate Use Act, Proposition 215, for medical use within a patients' collective; but once her neighbors threatened to call the authorities, she got nervous and shut down her operation. "That was good for me!" Aggrey says. "I wrote more, I felt less scared and at risk of going to jail. I did a lot of shit. I was a building manager, I painted rich people's houses, I still grew a little bit—you can't stop!" She bursts into a grin, a tiny Madonna-esque gap between her two front teeth.

We're sitting at a table in the light-drenched living room of the apartment she shares with her husband, author David Lida. Two spindly marijuana plants stretch

FEATURES

their leaves toward the window. "We are waiting on a referendum [in Mexico City] that will allow for up to 20 plants to be grown for personal consumption," she explains. "And if that passes, that's where I think marijuana can truly become radical. It becomes something for the people, for home and homeopathic use, removed from illegal and or commercial markets. It would be access for all," she says, patting their leaves. "I mean, it is just a frickin' plant."

After she shut the grow-op down, Aggrey moved back to the East Coast to be closer to family. The daughter of a Ghanaian-Liberian mother and a Liberian father who met and fell in love in New York City, Aggrey was born on Staten Island, and raised bouncing around Baltimore County and central Pennsylvania, out to the West Coast and back again. She settled in Brooklyn and found a job with Whoopi & Maya—the Whoopi Goldberg-backed company selling therapeutic cannabis products for women.

"At that time the cannabis industry was starting to morph into a legal, or semilegal space, where a lot of people were showcasing products, not quite selling, but trying to legitimize what it meant to be a user or a grower," Aggrey says. After a few years of brutal winters and feeling suffocated by the financial cramp of another American city, Aggrey was looking for what was next. "My partner at the time and I thought: maybe South Africa? Berlin? But Mexico City seemed closer and somewhat more approachable. I thought the culture shock would be less intense after living in Latinx California and in a sister country to the US." They moved south.

Carving out a space for herself took time. Mexico's relationship to drugs is fraught; movements toward legality are complicated by the violent shadow of narcotrafficking and a political system blighted by corruption. "Mexico is culturally conservative and you have to be a little more toned-down in all arenas of life—in the activities you do, with political activism, in dress and certainly with weed. It feels smarter to me to keep a low profile," Aggrey explains. She wears gold hoop earrings, her head shaved, and a disarming smile; it's hard to imagine her not being noticed in a crowd anywhere. "Yet, here we are! Holding on to dear life!"

In the US, many people remain incarcerated on marijuana charges that are no longer classed as criminal. "It's such bullshit," says Aggrey.

She recently joined Xula, a CBD firm focusing on women's cycles, as creative director. They are in beta, waiting on legislation, pressing on the impenetrable beast that is Mexican bureaucracy. "Right now, we have no idea what is happening," she says. "The mayor just declared that personal use is, or will shortly be, decriminalized, though growing and selling is still illegal. The government is supposedly writing legislation that will be finalized in... six months? A year? Who knows—it's Mexico. It takes 10 times as much time and effort to get anything done."

Waiting for things to happen is a common refrain here. In the meantime, Aggrey wrote a book. *The Art of Weed Butter*, published by Ulysses Press in January 2019, is a friendly guide to cooking with marijuana. "I wasn't planning on positioning myself as a food and recipe authority," she says, "but I had some experience cooking with and eating weed from Whoopi & Maya and some publishers hit me up. It was an opportunity to think of weed as not just recreational or medicinal but in terms of wellness—as an edible plant that nurtures and heals—and how we can make that more approachable to the modern user."

The cookbook was also an opportunity to dive deeper into her roots and to revisit the dishes she grew up eating, like cassava leaf and rice, jollof and fufu. Another arm of Aggrey's research and activism explores the culinary lineage of people and ingredients brought to Mexico during the transatlantic slave trade—a legacy that is largely absent from Mexican public discourse.

"I feel like a phony sometimes, not being a real authority on food. I am proud of the book and it feels good to have it out in the world, but the imposter syndrome is so real," she says. Her recipe for West African fried chicken features a marinade of cannabis-infused grapeseed oil, black pepper and chili pepper, which yields golden, shatteringly crisp chicken. It is with these recipes you glimpse Aggrey at her best: cooking and caring for others. "I hate the term 'ganjapreneur,' I don't use it," she says. "'Cannabis creative'? I guess? But I often call myself 'weed *tía*' [aunt]... you know, late 30s, ran around the industry for a while. I want it to come from a place of comfort, of nurturing." Our conversation turns to the very

*"The more we are aware of the disparity, the less people are able to blindly consume marijuana,
or start weed or CBD businesses, without being a part of this larger conversation."*

real sense of fear and instability for communities in crisis due to marijuana prosecution. "It's such bullshit," Aggrey says. "The fact that MedMen is on 5th Avenue, an elite dispensary making bank, and there's an accessory shop in Barneys selling to an uptown clientele, while you have young black men getting sent to Rikers for an attempt to sell." She is solemn. I ask, "What do we do about these structural inequalities? How do we support weed and weed use while this is still happening?" She fires back immediately, "Number one: We need to make sure that there are expunged records for all low-level marijuana prosecutions. Next, we need equity programs at every juncture of commerce; we need a more equal playing field and to provide resources to those undergoing prosecution or who have been locked up." It is by working within the industry that Aggrey aims to uncover and rectify the imbalance: "The more we are aware of this disparity, the less people are able to blindly con-

sume marijuana, or start weed or CBD businesses, or engage with weed in any meaningful way without being a part of this larger conversation, is key." She adds, "We have a lot of work to do."

For now, it's back to the nine-to-five. She stretches out her legs, capped with speckled horsehair boots. After work at Xula, there will be more work planning *Cenas Sin Fronteras* (dinners without borders), a benefit she is organizing. Inspired by a recent trip to the US-Mexico border where migrant caravans seeking asylum are stalled, the event is the perfect confluence of Aggrey's talents. "I realized that just going once to drop off a few boxes of tampons wasn't sufficient," she says. "I thought, what can I offer that people will pay money for so we can extend our reach?" A party that brings together community, activism, weed and Afro-Mexican flavors was born. "Let's throw all this shit together. That's all I can offer," she says as she clears the dishes to the sink.

The Furthest

Under the low-hanging orb of an alien landscape, first light and a strange awakening.

Dawn

Photography by Romain Laprade & Styling by Camille-Joséphine Teisseire

Anders wears a gilet and trousers by Lanvin and a sweater by Hermès.
Johanna wears a turtleneck by Sportmax, a skirt by Icicle and shoes by Martinez. Previous spread: Anders wears a blazer and trousers by Rochas.

Johanna wears a silk dress by Hermès. Anders wears a cashmere suit by Hermès and a turtleneck by MaxMara.

Anders wears trousers by De Fursac and a turtleneck by MaxMara. Johanna wears a dress by AMI Paris and shoes by Santoni.

RISING STARS

TEXT:
DEBIKA RAY

Until a few years ago, astrology sat alongside crystal balls and Ouija boards as an eccentric, outmoded form of spirituality. Now, horoscopes are a mainstay of online media, advice columns and even dating profiles. Debika Ray charts astrology's cosmic journey back into the popular consciousness and learns why a nonhierarchical, culturally inclusive system of belief makes perfect sense to so many.

Thank goodness someone thought to publish an online list of all the astrological signs represented as cat breeds. In case you're curious: Geminis are most like ragdolls, Libras may feel an affinity with the American shorthair and Scorpios are likely to identify with the brawny Maine coon.

For many people under 40, these comparisons will need little explanation. Like with so many age-old cultural phenomena, the internet has given new form to the venerable practice of astrology, a system that claims human events and personal characteristics can be explained and predicted by observing the movements of celestial bodies. A historic feature of practically every culture from China to Latin America, it had an almost scholarly status in the ancient world and continues to be referenced as part of everyday life in India and other countries. In the West, however, it has been relegated over time to the realm of "belief."

Today, "Mercury is in retrograde"—which describes a period in the cosmos when the planet nearest to the sun appears to be moving the wrong way across the sky—is a phrase that conjures panic in some and mirth in others. "When that's about to happen, my friend and I will batten down the hatches," says London-based Isabella Smith, who describes her belief in astrology as "simultaneously sincere and heavily jokey." She explains, "We actually believe in it, but also take it with a pinch of salt, which is common across my group of friends." Her interest in astrology sits alongside "a hodgepodge of spiritual beliefs," including reincarnation and the power of herbal medicine, and is even a factor in deciding who to date. "It makes sense to me to make space for more than what Western scientific thinking can offer—to have time for other traditions that aren't grounded in the material or the measurable."

Smith, 28, is not alone. Linda Woodhead, a professor in the department of politics, philosophy and religion at Lancaster University who lists the growth of alternative spiritualities among her interests, notes the particular popularity of astrology and horoscopes today among younger millennials. "There was a stereotype that it was the preserve of stupid, superstitious women, while mainstream religion was controlled by men and the politically privileged, but the stigma is being removed now, and it's becoming much more mainstream," she says. "I think astrology is attractive because it gives you a framework for understanding yourself, making sense of life and classifying people, as well as thinking about the future. In a world that hits younger people particularly as not having much structure, stability or certainty, that's obviously useful."

There isn't an easy way to track the shifting views toward astrology, and Woodhead says there is no concrete evidence to suggest there has been an overall rise in astrology in Western countries; it remains a constant but minority interest. But it's clear to the casual observer that it's trendy again in a way that hasn't been obvious since the peak of the New Age movement of the 1970s, when Western cultures embraced a range of heterodox spiritual traditions. As the freewheeling '70s gave way to the reactionary conservatism of the '80s, astrology was relegated to the back burner as a source of ridicule and light entertainment for most. Entertainment is now still a part of it (think zodiac memes), but the seriousness with which people treat astrology seems to be changing in some circles. Woodhead suggests that the zeitgeist for astrology today might chime with the rise in more plural, subjective modes of thinking, as the certainties and hierarchies of the late 20th century are crumbling. "It has to do with the decline in the prestige of one model of science and of experts having all the answers," she says. "Big, powerful men think, 'I'm in control of the world and I can make anything happen just by willing it,' whereas most of the rest of us think, 'No, I'm just a tiny little speck affected by wider forces that I haven't got much control over.' That worldview—away from the big acting ego and toward a more interconnected view of the world—makes more sense to most of us, and astrology is closer to that worldview."

The basic underlying premise that the wider cosmos influences and affects us, also appears to resonate with people in an era of ecological crisis. "We're increasingly aware of the limitations of what our current materialistic mindset can offer, and what it has done for us," says Smith. "It has done plenty of wonderful things, but it has also brought us imminent planetary meltdown. So there's a certain skepticism about the rationalist, scientific understanding of

the world, which hasn't always served us best." Beyond the memes and the speed with which new ideas can take hold, the internet has made astrology more accessible and inclusive because the complex calculations involved can be done at the touch of a button without consulting an expert. There are countless websites that take the date, time and location of your birth and instantly spit out your sun, rising and moon signs—information that can then be used to obtain much more detailed and personalized information than you could previously find in horoscope columns.

And a growing number of cutting-edge independent magazines now offer horoscopes. For example, Marissa Malik—who does readings for private clients—also writes a monthly column for *Gal-Dem*, a London-based publication written by women and nonbinary people of color. "People are taking it more seriously than they were even three years ago," she says. "People always have a need for spirituality, and astrology provides that in a way that's very individual and less preachy. It's a great way of having connectivity to people but you can also practice it on an individual basis."

Malik's interest in astrology was sparked when she was about 10 or 11, growing up in Connecticut in a culturally mixed household. Her

"It makes sense to me to make space for more than what Western scientific thinking can offer—to have time for other traditions that aren't grounded in the material or the measurable. We actually believe in it, but also take it with a pinch of salt."

father is Pakistani and her mother is Mexican, and while she was raised Roman Catholic, her grandmother practiced mysticism and Reiki. "I grew up in an environment where the fusing of different practices and cultures, alternative forms of thinking and an acceptance of multifaceted ideas around spirituality were always present," she says. While she practices astrology in the Western tradition, she's conscious of her South Asian heritage—a part of the world where birth charts and the movement of celestial bodies are routinely taken into account when making significant decisions.

Indeed, the multicultural nature of much of Western society and youth culture—facilitated by the internet and migration—is perhaps one reason that astrology has such a pull today. In ethnically diverse communities, Malik feels this is particularly important. "There's a propensity for diasporic people of color to have difficult relationships to spirituality," she says. "If you've been displaced or moved, you may have connections to a culture where spirituality is really strong, while being embedded in Western culture, too. Horoscopes present a kind of cross between the two."

The nonhierarchical, nonjudgmental and nondogmatic nature of the belief system as compared to many more conventional reli-

gions may be why astrology seems to attract people who identify as queer, or those who may have faced discrimination in some way. "I don't think I've given a reading to a cisgender man in at least nine months and a lot of my client base are people who have a lot of turmoil in their lives," says Malik. "I think this may be related to a mistrust among those who have been mistreated by the system, and a willingness to understand that answers can come from different places at a time when fascism is on the rise again and pressure is being put on marginalized groups."

Woodhead is not convinced by the idea that astrology holds a special appeal for disempowered people, but agrees that in Western societies it has long been attractive to marginalized groups. In the modern era it has been associated with women, who have tended to have less access to the levers of power and relied instead on their interpersonal skills. As a result of this association, astrology has been stigmatized in a way that mainstream religion—dominated by men—hasn't been. She speculates that the seeming appeal of astrology to the LGBT community today may have similar roots. "Maybe it's a useful tool for people who are already thinking hard about what it is to be human," she says. Smith's assertion that she takes astrology with

a pinch of salt may also help explain its relevance today—not just as a belief structure but as a mode of relating to others. As Woodhead says: "It's not that people know for certain it is absolutely true. They can be a bit skeptical—laugh and joke about it. You can dismiss it, but it's still a point of social contact that's fun and entertaining, much like talking about football."

Woodhead makes another observation that sheds light on the role of astrology in contemporary life: "It's not dissimilar to how people of the same generation play with, for example, Harry Potter characters—you can identify as a Gryffindor or as a Hermione." This comparison to literature can be a useful way to conceptualize astrology: Humans have long turned to stories to make sense of the world, using the narrative arc and relationships between characters to interpret the narrative landscape of our own lives, and then rewriting it if we choose. For many people, horoscopes appear to operate similarly, except more like a "choose your own adventure" novel or a video game—a personalized story to reflect on, and then accept or reject. Seen in that light, they don't feel too far from mainstream religious texts, which today are rarely taken literally. If both these and horoscopes offer universal truths, who really cares if they are true?

At Work With: Ormaie

Can you bottle a family memory, and would anybody else want to smell it if you could? **Annick Weber meets the** mother-and-son duo intent on finding out. Photography by *Christian Møller Andersen*

Ormaie is the French term for a grove of elm trees—a nod to the perfume makers' insistence on all-natural ingredients.

Nothing conjures memories like a scent. The smell of flowers might fill one person with echoes of childhood summers. For someone else, it might cast the mind back to far-flung holidays. This nostalgia is a key ingredient in the fragrances dreamed up by Marie-Lise Jonak and Baptiste Bouygues, the mother-and-son duo behind the all-natural French perfume brand Ormaie. "If you want people to feel something, you have to turn to what has marked you the most," says Bouygues. "All our inspirations come from the places and people we have known."

To smell the seven fragrances that make up the Ormaie collection is to flick through a family album. Bouygues and Jonak have spent much of their lives in the same homes. They also attended the same school in rural France, albeit a generation apart, and vacationed at the same summer houses in the south of the country. "When you work in perfume with a family member, it is natural that you have many common references because you have an identical olfactive history," explains Bouygues. He takes a tester strip from a drawer in Ormaie's Paris office and sprays it with Papier Carbone, a spice-and-wood-layered fragrance evoking Bouygues and Jonak's childhood classroom, with hints of carbon paper, wood-paneled libraries and licorice eaten in the schoolyard. After a minute or so he passes the strip to his mother and the two of them sit with their eyes closed to enhance the enjoyment of the scent.

"Our characters are very complementary, which makes working together easy," explains Jonak, who, like her son, is soft-spoken and attentive. "There's no competition. You know that what the other person is doing is in the best interest of both of us." Their relationship has only deepened since they officially launched Ormaie in November 2018. "Basically, this is the first time we've hung out," Bouygues jokes. For over 25 years, Jonak was working as a fragrance consultant to global brands, which regularly took her away from home for extended periods. Bouygues spent those weeks living with his grandparents, Jonak's parents. His mother would come back from trips with her bags filled to bursting. "Our home was packed with bottles of fragrances," recalls Jonak. "I was constantly testing things on my family, neighbors or my hairdresser to get their opinion on a new scent."

PERFUMES ARE COMPOSED
ENTIRELY OF NATURAL
INGREDIENTS AND THEIR
COLOUR MAY CHANGE OVER
TIME. THIS WILL NOT AFFECT
THEIR SCENT.

ORMAIE

COMP

Voyage
Sac
E7v7

OSÉ

AU NATUREL

by Harriet Fitch Little

Natural perfumes have flourished as part of the recent boom in clean beauty—the movement away from synthetic ingredients such as parabens and phthalates often used in makeup and skincare. (Research conducted by one natural deodorant company concluded that the average woman applies over 500 chemicals to her skin on a daily basis.) Of course, synthetic ingredients are popular for a reason: They have a longer shelf life and the resulting formulas can be far more uniform. Natural perfumes like Ormaie will vary slightly over time, just like wine would according to vintage, and must be applied more regularly. *Photography: Vingt-deux Paris*

As a young boy surrounded by a kaleidoscope of smells, Bouygues would dedicate his free time to making rose essence from the flowers picked in his grandmother's garden. Or he would sit with his grandfather, watching him make sculptures from freshly cut wood—a scent that, for him, is akin to the Proustian madeleine. "I've always wanted to found a *maison*, where generations of one family could share their creativity," explains Bouygues. "I love this type of know-how, this way of going through a lot of time and effort to make great things together." And so in spring 2016, while working in fashion communications in Europe and Asia, Bouygues told his mother about an idea he had been playing with for some time: to join forces and reclaim the craft of making non-synthetic, 100% natural fragrances.

Bouygues' proposal was met by Jonak with skepticism. Decades of professional experience had taught her that all great modern perfumes were built on synthetic molecules because they "bring a softness that people are accustomed to." Obtaining that same effect from all-natural components was going to be a complex task, one that the perfumers already in her orbit told her was impossible. "It took a long time, but finally we managed to find a group of perfumers who were really passionate about raw materials and ready to take on the challenge," says Jonak. "They had to know what naturals to replace the synthetics with. Otherwise, you risk ending up with an unbalanced composition that feels like it has holes between its top, middle and base notes."

Patience and dedication play a central role in all Bouygues and Jonak do. The mixing process, for example, involves waiting up to five weeks between trials as smells can take weeks to develop; when using synthetic components, this is a five-minute procedure. While Jonak liaises with stockists and the perfumers in Grasse, Bouygues travels all across France to visit flower fields and producers, commission typography for the Imprimerie du Marais–printed labels and meet the craftsmen behind the sculptural perfume bottles, which are made from 30% recycled glass and beechwood sourced from renewable forests. But for Bouygues and Jonak, the care put into every step of the process pays for itself: "You can feel the people cultivating the flowers in each of our fragrances," Bouygues says. "This is what makes them poetic. They touch you in a way that is more deeply linked to memories and feelings. Try comparing the experience of eating an apricot ice pop to that of biting into a real apricot, freshly picked from a tree; they are nothing like each other."

What people feel when smelling an Ormaie fragrance is firmly rooted in their own personal history. Although inspired by a Tuscan landscape under the morning mist, the citrusy-gingery cologne Les Brumes also reminds Jonak of the lemon-scented soap used on the trains from a bygone era, long before Bouygues was born. "Sometimes we disagree on what exactly it is that we smell, but the overall story is always the same," Jonak chuckles. Other scents, like the fresh floral 28 Degrees, waft you away to a summer evening in the South of France, just when the scorching heat begins to fade, the air smelling of orange blossoms, jasmine and the remains of sunscreen on warm skin.

Two of the Ormaie fragrances are particularly close to Bouygues and Jonak's hearts for their direct link to family members. Le Passant, a classic cologne with top notes of lavender and bergamot, was made in honor of Bouygues' father, who wore a similar fragrance. "It's the perfume that took the longest to make, because I didn't want to compromise on this memory," he explains. The second one, Ormaie's take on a classic feminine fragrance, is named after Jonak's mother, Yvonne, referencing the rose and red fruit bushes from her garden. "We wanted it to be a timeless fragrance that both my mother and daughter could wear," says Jonak. "Yvonne found herself feeling really young when she first smelled it," Bouygues laughs, explaining that his grandmother keeps asking for more bottles of the perfume to give to her friends: "She's so proud, all the grandmas in the village are now wearing Yvonne." For a maison rooted in family values, there can be no better seal of approval than that.

Although certain fragrances used in Ormaie perfumes might be more associated with traditionally male or female scents, the range is intended to be unisex.

The first perfumers in Grasse started growing roses on behalf of local tanneries, who used them to mask the bad odor of their gloves.

Bea

In 1962, two young assistants ascended to one of the top spots in magazine design. *Katie Calautti* charts *Ruth Ansel* and *Bea Feitler*'s groundbreaking collaboration at *Harper's Bazaar,* without which the '60s might never have swung quite so hard.

Ruth.

&

The history-making collaboration between Ruth Ansel and Bea Feitler came about as the result of a bitter argument.

In 1962, *Harper's Bazaar* art director Marvin Israel was fired on the spot by Editor-in-Chief Nancy White, after he commissioned a cover featuring a model who looked exactly like the magazine's iconic former fashion editor, Diana Vreeland—a heavy-handed insinuation that Vreeland should have been given the top job.

At that moment, Israel's two 24-year-old assistants, Ruth Ansel and Bea Feitler, assumed his role, becoming the first-ever female art directors of *Harper's Bazaar*, and the youngest in the industry. It was the first of many firsts for both women, who were about to change the print design world forever.

The two arrived at their jobs in diametrically different ways. Feitler, born in Rio de Janeiro to Jewish parents who fled Nazi Germany, studied at Parsons School of Design in New York City. After graduation, she returned to Brazil where she worked for the pro-

gressive literary magazine *Senhor* before moving back to New York in 1961 and accepting a job at *Bazaar* as an assistant to Israel, her former Parsons professor. Ansel, meanwhile, was born in the Bronx and studied fine art at Alfred University before being introduced to graphic design by her then-husband, Bob Gill. Shortly after Feitler was hired, Ansel landed an interview with Israel. "Although I didn't have a graphic design portfolio, he decided to take a risk and hire me anyway," Ansel once told *Creative Review*. "He liked the idea that I didn't have to unlearn graphic design clichés."

"They put us together because it bought them time to shop around and look for a male art director to replace us," Ansel explained to *Creative Review*, recalling her and Feitler's status after Israel's departure. "They never told us that, but we suspected it. But once they discovered that we weren't doing such a bad job, they kept us on. One of the factors that weighted in our favor was that we came pretty cheap. Our combined salary was probably less than an established male

art director earned at the time." They wasted no time in upending much more than merely sexist stereotypes. "This is a theory," says Paula Scher, a partner at design studio Pentagram. "I think because they were women, and they were outside the group of famous men, they were capable of breaking rules and trying things. They didn't have to adhere to the same standards men did because no one had the expectation they would."

"Bea and Ruth truly complemented each other," says artist and researcher Nicolau Vergueiro. "Being looked at skeptically for being young women in power positions, I think Bea and Ruth, as a duo, allowed each other to be as bold and daring as they could: the power of two." Along with infusing *Bazaar* with their seemingly boundless youthful energy, Feitler and Ansel also fostered new talent. Photographers Bill King, Diane Arbus, Duane Michals, Bill Silano and Bob Richardson blossomed under their collaborative efforts. Their work throughout their decade-long tenure has come to be seen as quintessential visual representations of a rapidly changing era. This was the decade where space travel, television, plastic surgery and boundary-pushing fashion was on everyone's lips. Gloria Guinness wrote about pornography and the pill within *Bazaar*'s pages. Women wanted feminist commentary on sex, marriage and careers—they were starting to expect more from their fashion magazines—and Feitler and Ansel were all too happy to serve it to them on a Day-Glo platter. They cut and glued and juxtaposed into *Bazaar*'s pages the vitality they experienced on the streets of swinging '60s New York City: freshly emancipated youth, pop art,

Throughout their careers, the designers clung to Ansel's belief that you should "always hire people smarter than you." They both sought to encourage new styles of expression among students— including, in Feitler's case—that of a young Keith Haring.

"They put us together because it bought them time to look for a male art director to replace us."

rock music and classic cinema. Feitler and Ansel filled the ever-changing wall in their office with torn-out images and photos, using it as a hub of invention. "They were open to accidents, material around the studio, and events surrounding them," graphic designer Philip B. Meggs once wrote for the American Institute of Graphic Arts, of their process. "We were sometimes competitive and often tried to top each other, which kept us on our toes," Ansel told *Creative Review*. "In the end our work became seamless and inevitably our concepts spilled over into each other's work."

1965 was a year of major milestones for the duo. The February issue featured actor Steve McQueen as the cover model, marking the first time a man graced the front of any major women's fashion magazine. Model Jean Shrimpton's bracelet-sheathed arm cradling McQueen's face is still one of the most replicated images born of Ansel and Feitler's direction. They also featured supermodel Donyale Luna in the April issue—the first time a black model was pictured in an American fashion magazine.

That April 1965 "Pop" issue remains Ansel and Feitler's best-known achievement at Bazaar. To this day, it's considered a landmark in both design and content, capturing the dazzling anticipation of the mid-1960s. Aimed at being "a partial passport to the off-beat side of Now," the issue was guest-edited by photographer Richard Avedon. The cover features Shrimpton—the red-hot model of the moment—in a pink cutout space helmet. Some versions even incorporated lenticular technology that made Shrimpton's eye appear to blink.

The creation of that now-iconic cover was a last-ditch, late-night decision. Shrimpton had been shot by Avedon in a hat that everyone hated. As the print deadline passed, "Ruth started to explain that we could cut the shape of the space helmet out of Day-Glo paper," Avedon wrote in a 1968

Graphics piece. "But she never finished because Bea was already cutting... It all happened in minutes—the moment was absolute magic, to watch Bea, the classicist, and Ruth, the modern, work as if they were one person." Though the April 1965 issue was a commercial failure, it won the coveted New York Art Directors Club medal and is heralded as an enduring emblem of the '60s.

Despite their professional accolades, once new editorial leadership arrived at *Bazaar* in 1971, the co-art directors were pushed out. "We became pressured when the magazine lost some of its readership," Feitler once explained in a 1977 *Graphics Today* interview.

In 1972, Feitler joined Gloria Steinem's newly launched *Ms.* magazine as art director, then moved on to *Rolling Stone*. In 1978, she created the look for Condé Nast's new publication *Self*, and in 1981, she began redesigning the premiere issue of *Vanity Fair*'s revival. But she never saw it published—she was diagnosed with a rare form of cancer and passed away in 1982 at the age of 44.

In addition to her magazine work, Feitler had also been a teacher and mentor. "In the late 1970s she used to say she wanted to come back to Brazil and teach design and art direction here," says her nephew Bruno Feitler, who published a book about his aunt in 2012. "Teaching was very inspirational for her."

"She had an eye for talented people and found and nurtured them," says Paula Greif, who was Feitler's student at the School of Visual Arts and her assistant in the mid-1970s. Greif later became the art director of *Mademoiselle*. "There is a whole generation who can say Bea Feitler gave them their first job." Annie Leibovitz called Feitler her first great mentor. In fact, Leibovitz's move to fashion was Feitler's doing—she introduced the photographer to *Vanity Fair*, which kicked off a storied partnership.

Ansel, who was the first female art director at *The New York Times*

"It was magic to watch Bea, the classicist, and Ruth, the modern, work as if they were one person."

The style that came to be associated with Ansel and Feitler was defined by their daring and spontaneity. Some of their most striking covers were made by experimenting with graphic shapes, either achieved through photographic tricks such as the foregrounding of legs on the August 1966 cover (bottom) made to accompany a feature about tights, or through collage, as in the case of the iconic yet commercially unsuccessful April 1965 Jean Shrimpton cover (top). They were also open to eye-catching advances in print: Versions of the April 1965 cover incorporated a form of lenticular technology that made Shrimpton's long-lashed blue eye appear to blink, a technologically-advanced format that further pushed the boundaries of Feitler and Ansel's collage design.. *Top Photograph by Richard Avedon © The Richard Avedon Foundation*

Magazine in the 1970s, followed by stints at *Vogue* and *House & Garden*, was asked to build on Feitler's vision at *Vanity Fair* as its first female art director. "It felt strange. I felt very conflicted about it," Ansel explained to *Creative Review*. "I didn't expect it and I didn't quite know how to handle it. But I did it because I couldn't say no." After almost a decade working with Editor-in-Chief Tina Brown to create an iconic record of the Hollywood-obsessed 1980s, Ansel formed her own design studio in 1992, where she continues to work to this day. Some of her designs include ad campaigns for Versace and Karl Lagerfeld and books for Annie Leibovitz, Peter Beard and Elsa Peretti.

As with many previously unheralded women, Ansel and Feitler's work is experiencing a renewed public fascination. In 2009, Ansel was the subject of the first in a series of books highlighting female graphic designers called *Hall of Femmes*. And Nicolau Vergueiro has championed Feitler's work since 2017 through a touring exhibition that has shown in Berlin, Oslo and Cologne. "Feitler was part of creating new standards in publication that are still current," he says. "In *Ms.*, her work lays out aesthetics of punk and zine culture, which in turn points to blogs and webpages. In *Rolling Stone*, she mastered the overlay of images to convey documentarist pictorial essays, a convention in contemporary visual design."

"The great art director Bea Feitler taught me the value of stopping from time to time and looking back at one's work," Leibovitz wrote in her book *Annie Leibovitz: Portraits 2005-2016*. "She said that you learn the most from your own work, and by looking back you find how you need to go forward." Perhaps it is our newfound interest in looking back—particularly at the women who quietly shaped their industries—that is allowing Ansel and Feitler's names to finally be placed among the giants of magazine design.

Photograph: Bea Feitler Portrait (1960s) by Bob Richardson. Courtesy of The New School Archives and Special Collection, The New School, New York, NY.

Home Tour:
The New Palace

In a sleepy city in western Gujurat, *Komal Sharma* discovers the last maharaja of Morvi's extravagant art deco playground. Photography by *Salva López* & Production by *Vinay Panjwani*

Four hours west of Ahmedabad, along a spectacularly straight road dotted with occasional settlements, sits one of India's most surprising architectural masterpieces: a maharaja's palace designed to conform to the purest precepts of art deco style.

When it was built in 1942, the palace represented a radical shift from traditional palace architecture of the time. Perhaps that's why its owner, Thakur Mahendrasinh, christened it the New Palace. He was the last maharaja of Morvi—a town which, historically, was a principality ruled by the warrior clan of Jadeja Rajputs. As remote as the New Palace feels geographically, it is a building firmly situated in the pivots of history. In the 1940s, when British colonizers still ruled, India's royal families felt themselves slipping between past grandeur and a new sense of nationalism.

A generation of princes and princesses had been sent to the United Kingdom to study; they flirted with living in Europe and the US, where they had witnessed the West's burgeoning architectural modernism. Art deco took hold in India all through the mid-20th century, particularly in the port hub of Mumbai. Local architectural historians claim it has one of the world's largest concentrations of art deco buildings, second only to Miami. Thakur Mahendrasinh took the fashion for art deco to the biggest canvas possible: a brand new palace designed by architects Gregson Batley & King—a British firm popular in Mumbai—and constructed by Shapoorji Pallonji, also responsible for iconic projects including the Bombay Stock Exchange and Hong Kong Bank.

Rajkumari Rukshmani Devi, the daughter of the late Thakur Mahendrasinh, recalls her father's vision fondly. "It was the dream of a young maharaja," writes the former princess, who is known colloquially as Mira Ba. "In his early 20s, my father had traveled to America and he became very interested in art deco. It was the fashion at the time."

The New Palace, a two-story structure with perfectly rounded edges on two corners, sits square in the center of a massive estate (the palace itself occupies only a tenth of the site). The cylindrical columns that line its facade give the exterior the quintessential geometry of art deco. I enter through the main door, into a terrazzo corridor that runs along the building's periphery. Rows and rows of elaborately furnished drawing and dining rooms peel off from the corridor, enclosing the two open inner courtyards with fountains. The New Palace brings together the best of European modernism with traditional Indian typologies such as these cooling central spaces.

But it is in its interiors, furnishing, art and artifacts, that Morvi's palace comes to life. It is, without a doubt, a young man's indulgence. The memories of decadent

The New Palace is maintained by a permanent staff, many of whom have lived there for decades. A flag is raised when the royal family is in residence.

The art deco movement was heavily influenced by the era's interest in the decorative art of the Far East, an interplay which adds another layer of complexity to the palace's interiors.

Furnishings for the palace were shipped from an upmarket interiors firm headquartered on London's Tottenham Court Road.

parties echo in its halls, lounges and grand staircase. In a more remote corner of the palace is an opulent bar with leopard-print upholstery, mirror work and erotic murals showing light-skinned women alongside darker-skinned men and women, all of them indulging in a garden of plenty. The maharaja commissioned Polish artist Stefan Norblin to decorate this palace, and his work ranges between seductive flapper-era portraits and mythological scenes of Shiva and Krishna.

The delight is in the details. There's an indoor swimming pool with an attached gymnasium of curious contraptions, followed by a library that is right out of an English townhouse, complete with walnut wood paneling and a fireplace. Ahead, in an office stuffed with books and papers, Manharsinh, the palace's caretaker since 1981, pulls out An Estimate of Decorations and Furnishing,

an exhaustive proposal sent from Tottenham Court Road in London, all the way to this remote corner of Gujarat.

The list is long, descriptive and evidence of a discerning taste for luxury. "Napoleon marble columns, Botticino marble linings and architraves to the doorway, Cedar onyx columns with Belgian Bleu marble plinths, sliding doors cellulosed in Cheltenham bronze, satin silver electric ceiling pendants with 28 inch diameter glass bowls and clear glass rods and glass leaves, chairs in Cuban mahogany, pedestals in French Walnut, Island settee with vermin proof upholstery, first-class springing and stuffing, and covered in material to selection…" The list goes on.

"The maharaja loved all beautiful things, be it homes, artifacts, art," writes Mira Ba. "He was a good tennis and polo player. His absolute, true love was horses. He

was an excellent rider and raced all over the world. He was a keen golfer and wanted to build a golf course in Morvi. He also built an airport in Morvi and kept a small plane." Relics of these hobbies live on at the New Palace: The walls are bedecked with trophies and medallions, oil canvases of horse riders and polo players, and larger-than-life portraits of ancestors including his father, Lakhdhirji Bahadur, and grandfather, Waghji Bahadur, dressed in all their finery. Modernity and tradition lie next to each other here, playfully and harmoniously.

As much as the New Palace is a story of the aesthetic, cultural and political shifts in the history of India, at its heart, it is someone's home. It feels unlived in, but not abandoned. Amidst all the elaborate furnishings, wall-to-wall carpeting, cabinets full of crockery and innumerable sofas and settees placed around mother-of-pearl

"It was the dream of a young maharaja. My father had traveled to America and he became very interested in art deco. It was the fashion."

Polish artist Stefan Norblin fled the Nazi occupation and became one of the most popular palace artists in India.

tables, once in a while, one spots vignettes of family life—photographs of young children or portraits of the women of the house, casually smiling at the camera, draped in elegant saris and pearl necklaces.

The palace is painstakingly maintained by a staff who have lived here and taken care of this property for all their lives, and they speak of it with tenderness. "When the royal family comes to live here, we hoist a flag on top, so that the town knows that they are home," says one. "I have grown up looking at these trees in this property; the mango, champa, have all grown with me," says another. The family, consisting currently of the queen and her four daughters, live in their various homes around the world, including Mumbai and London. They return to Morvi occasionally, along with their extended families, to the home of their childhood. Mira Ba says that the spirit of the place endures: "My father built this house for his mother, his wife, his children and himself," she writes. "It is home to us all no matter where we go. When we return, that's where all our love lies. In Morvi."

The family photos dotted around the palace are a reminder that this remains a family home—albeit only on holidays.

3
Intimacy

E S

Words by *Pip Usher*, Photography by *Katie McCurdy* & Styling by *Ashley Abtahie*

T H

Psychotherapist *Esther Perel* wants to fix your love life, but first she needs to change how you think about love.

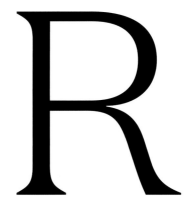

Couples who seek help when in crisis come to idolize the therapist who guides them out of it. Through her books, podcast and talks, *Esther Perel* has come to occupy that position in the hearts of millions. *Pip Usher* meets the psychotherapist whose unconventional understanding of intimacy is saving relationships around the world.

"Anybody who has lost someone knows that you can fall in love again."

"We have a new Olympus that we all want to climb and we don't necessarily have the tools to climb it," explains Antwerp-born psychotherapist Esther Perel in her trademark purr. The "Olympus" to which she refers encompasses the aspirations of modern-day relationships—on which Perel has emerged as a leading authority. In addition to her New York City private practice, her two bestselling books, *Mating in Captivity: Unlocking Erotic Intelligence* (which has evolved into an online course, *Rekindling Desire*) and *The State of Affairs: Rethinking Infidelity* have endeared Perel to a global audience seeking guidance. Her latest foray is her most daring yet: *Where Should We Begin?* is a podcast that invites listeners into an unscripted therapy session between Perel and an anonymous couple in crisis. While their stories are singular, their struggles—with betrayal, desire and loss—offer an unflinching insight into the hurdles of contemporary intimacy. Here, Perel lays out the pitfalls and pressures that now come with romantic relationships, and presents her clear-eyed road map for coming "back to life" as a couple.

PU: *We seem to be in a paradoxical age where we've become increasingly connected yet more and more lonely. What's been the impact of this shift upon our romantic relationships?* **EP:** We've never had more expectations from our romantic relationships than we do today. One could say that romanticism is a new religion and there's a conflation between our relationship needs and our spiritual needs. As Jungian analyst Robert Johnson says, we're looking to romantic love for what we used to look for in the realm of the divine, which is transcendence and meaning and purpose and ecstasy. We want everything that stability and commitment and trust and belonging and anchoring provide, but we want the same relationship to also provide us with awe and mystery and excitement and novelty. That combination—plus the traditional needs of a family—somebody to raise your kids with, sign your checks with, share family life with and go visit your parents with—is an amazingly long list. And it doesn't get shorter, it actually keeps getting longer.

PU: *Why are we now attaching this lengthy laundry list of needs and desires to our relationship?* **EP:** We used to live within clearly defined structures. People had tight knots and the knots were difficult to undo and therefore everybody knew their place, their role and what was expected of them. Today, we've shifted from structure to network—and networks are loosely tied knots which you can come in and out of really easily. When you have

that kind of fragmentation and atomization, your partner becomes the bulwark against the vicissitudes of life. They become the balm against the increasing existential isolation. And my claim has always been that people need community. No one person can sustain this, and relationships often crumble under the weight of expectations. Were those failures? Maybe not—maybe they actually accomplished more than many, many relationships of the past—but the list of expectations was so big that it looks like they didn't succeed.

PU: *What are the symptoms of a couple in trouble?* **EP:** Couples suffer because they are too enmeshed and in chronic friction, or because they are so far apart that the gap between them is too big. There's either too much reactivity or too little. At these extremes, people will either feel like they're suffocating—that they can't take a step alone and they have no sovereignty and no sense of autonomy whatsoever without eliciting reactivity from the other person—or they will be so far apart that they feel completely disconnected.

PU: *How do you differentiate between a rocky period and a relationship that's died?* **EP:** All people, like the moon, have intermittent eclipses. They forget or are somewhat distant, or they are a bit taken with other things that are demanding their full attention. They get pulled. But the difference between couples who have energy and are alive, versus couples who are dead, is that they catch themselves and acknowledge it. They reinfuse new energy, new attention, focus, presence and initiative into the relationship so that it revitalizes itself.

[A relationship has died] when curiosity is completely gone, when there is indifference, when there is complacency, when there is a chronic lack of appreciation and in turn when there is chronic criticism. It's not just the apathy, it's a deep lack of interest in the other person. People feel degraded when they are next to somebody who is utterly uninterested in them, and only interested in what they can provide. The functions have become more important than the people: the roles they inhabit, the things they take care of, the stuff they're in charge of. The relationship becomes massively practical and there's less of an interest in more existential questions. Who is this person whose heart is beating next to me? What's happening to them? What are they about, what are we about, where are we going, what's on your mind these days, what keeps you awake at night, what do you worry about, what brings you tremendous joy?

Hair: Yohey Nakatsuka, Makeup: Katie Mellinger, Photo Assistant: Austin Sandhaus, Personal Assistant: Samantha Lajoie

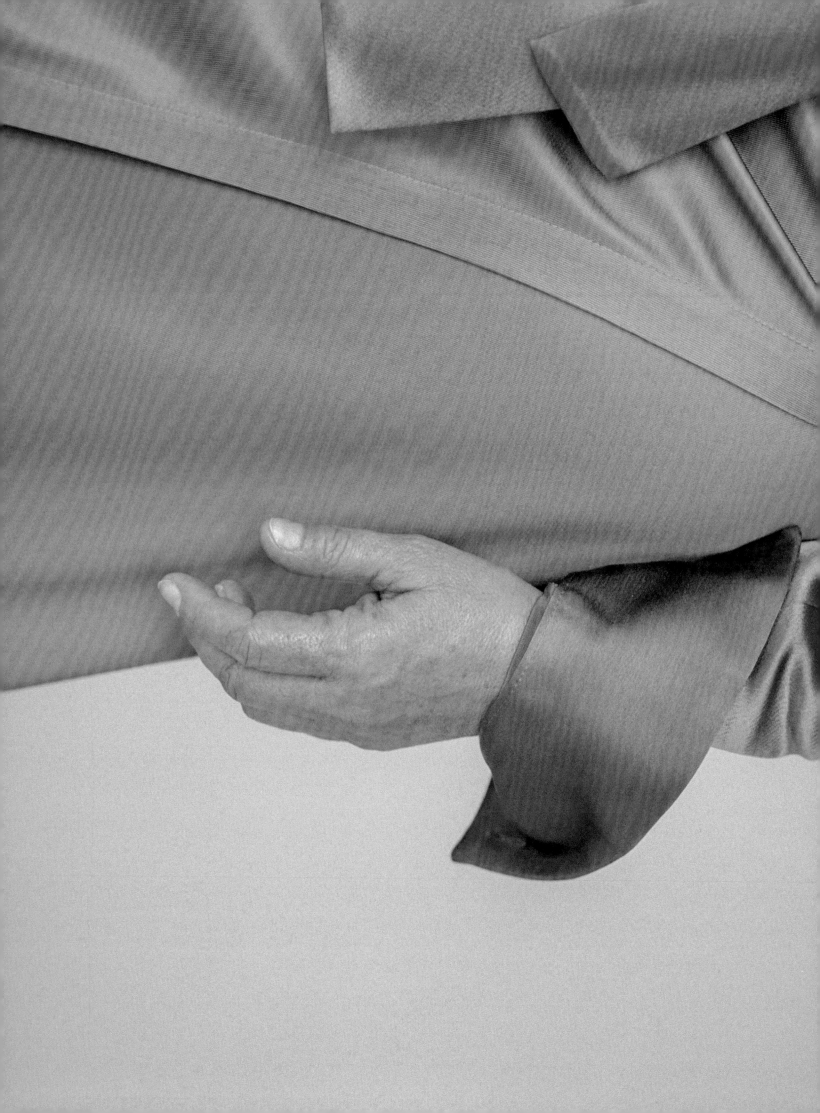

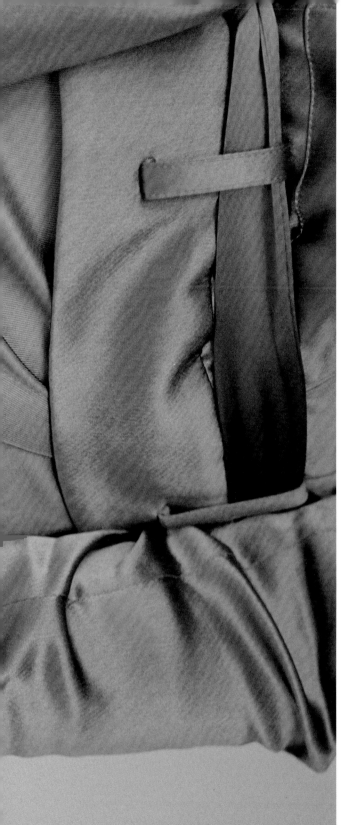

PU: *As a therapist, how do you help couples restore intimacy?* **EP:** If I want this car to drive, I need gasoline in the tank. The gasoline can be fear of loss, fear of being alone—I don't care what it is, but I do need to feel that there is a motivation of some sort to improve things. It doesn't have to be because you're deeply in love with this person. The love will follow when you feel that you laugh more together, that you share more together, that you get along and you're interested in each other, that you don't just feel like you're some kind of cooking machine or bank dispenser.

The degree to which a couple can still come back to life, revive and potentially even thrive, is determined by how they respond to the intervention that you give them. For those that are too close, it's about creating a degree of separateness and sovereignty, and for those who are so far apart and indifferent to each other, it's about creating a sense of empathy and curiosity. The degree to which they can do it—or not—is what tells you how much space for change and growth there is in the relationship.

PU: *What is the most damaging misconception about love?* **EP:** This mandate of "the one and only." Anybody who has lost someone knows that you can fall in love again. In the same way that we can love more than one child, we can love more than one person. After we mourn, and we grieve, there will be another person. And it will never be the same—it will be something else—but there isn't one person only.

PU: *What about sex?* **EP:** This kind of "swept away, suddenly I'm into it" spontaneity is an amazing myth. Committed sex is premeditated sex: It's willful, it's intentional, it's highly planned. If you wait for it to just happen, it won't. When you want to play tennis, you need to get your racket and ball, you need to reserve your court and you need to call somebody to play with. Nobody challenges the ritual of the preparation and the warm-up. Nobody suddenly just finds themselves on a court.

PU: *How do you reconcile differing sex drives in a relationship?* **EP:** You don't know if it's biological, hormonal, if there's a physiological component, if it's the context of life ("I'm exhausted, I have three young children"), if it's resentment ("You're not helping me"), if you're a selfish lover ("Last time you didn't ask me what I liked, of course I'm not interested"), if it's because they don't like their body therefore they have negative anticipation. Or if there are issues around lack of entitlement and the ability to be given to, to feel worthy of receiving, to experience pleasure. Discrepancy of desire is a symptom and, like every symptom, to understand it you have to look at the chronic condition. The chronic condition is: How do I relate to myself, how do I relate to you and how do we relate to each other?

PU: *If a couple wants to share their erotic thoughts, how do they open that conversation?* **EP:** A sexual fantasy articulates our deepest emotional needs that we bring to sex. That's the most important thing to understand: They are emotional scripts played out in the language of sex. I want to be ravished, I want to be irresistible, I want somebody who never says no to me. Or I want somebody who says "No, no, no" and finally says "Yes," meaning I am somebody who is able to change your mind, I am able to feel so powerful, so heroic. Every fantasy can pretty much be translated—it's like an architecture of psychological details.

The erotic mind knows very well to detect censorship and judgment and if it feels misunderstood, it just will stay in hiding. It won't say, "I like this," because it knows you will say, "Ugh." Some couples are able to share their erotic imaginations and erotic musings with each other. And with others, they don't. They go through a set of motions but they don't share an inner experience, which is the difference between sex and eroticism. The erotic is what gives meaning to sex; it's the poetics of it.

Perel is the daughter of Holocaust survivors who both lost their entire families. She says she owes much of her perspective on relationships to them—and their determination to embrace life fully.

"The erotic is what gives meaning to sex; it's the poetics of it."

PU: *Are there ways to maintain desire for your partner even as you're going through all the demands of life together?* **EP:** People need to understand that desire is not the only door through which you enter into a sexual interaction with your partner. Erotic couples understand that sometimes it's maintenance, sometimes it's beautiful high-production, sometimes it's arousal, sometimes its willingness and sometimes it's desire. You don't always get turned on just because you're looking at your partner; your own awakening takes place in multiple different things that have to do with your fantasy life and curiosity. And you remain responsive. This is very important—it's why I say spontaneity is a myth. You get turned on by being responsive to someone who comes toward you. You don't have to be turned on before they've even started. You basically experience a responsiveness and, through the responsiveness, your desire and your arousal follow.

That's particularly important for women to understand because the idea is that if you don't initiate, you're not in the mood. Moods come. "I'm not hungry, but I saw you eat—and I'm sitting next to you and it smells really nice so I take a taste, but I'm not really hungry and I say I'm not hungry, but at the same time I'm tasting it, and then I take a little plate, and then I take a bigger piece." It's that willingness to enter into a much more ambiguous zone, rather than yea or nay, I'm in the mood or I'm not in the mood.

PU: *You've challenged the belief that only unhappy people cheat by suggesting that an affair can be about recapturing a lost part of ourselves. Can you tell me more?* **EP:** Sometimes people realize that for the last 15 years all they've done is be parents and take care of the kids and they kind of just say, "This is the first time I can do something for myself and I don't know how to do this in the context of my family." These are not philanderers, these are not cheaters—these are people who are dealing with a sense of loss of who they once were, of what they once experienced, of what they hoped they could feel again. And they don't see home as a place for that.

Sometimes they are looking for that thing because there is a person next to them who has been basically unresponsive. They stand next to them, and lie next to them, and that person is just not responding. How many more years do they live like this? They just want to be touched, loved, kissed, adored, made love to, you name it. We're not talking about two months—we're talking about decades. Decades of sexual deserts. I think we have to understand the loneliness that people experience. It's not just that they're horny, it's way deeper. Erotic deadness is not just about not having sex. It's the loss of a whole dimension of oneself.

PU: *Is it possible to have a rewarding relationship without sex?* **EP:** For some people, sex is not really the place where they express themselves. It's not interesting to them. As long as both people are okay with it, then they have a perfectly rich relationship. I do think touch matters, though. Physicality matters, physical intimacy matters, but it doesn't always have to be sexual physical intimacy.

Perel's first viral article, "In Search of Erotic Intelligence," was published in 2002 as a response to the Clinton-Lewinsky affair.

Close

An illustration of the struggle to maintain personal boundaries in public spaces.

Enough

Photography by Ted Belton & Styling by Nadia Pizzimenti

Above: Samara wears a blouse by Bottega Veneta, a skirt by Maison Simons, boots by Fendi and eyewear by Andy Wolf. Madison wears a sweater and suit by COS and shoes by Hermès. Left: Madison wears a coat by Hermès. Samara wears a coat by Chloé and a hat by Maison Simons. Previous spread: Madison wears a top by Beaufille and earrings from Carole Tanenbaum Vintage Collection. Samara wears a sweater and tank top by 3.1 Phillip Lim.

Madison wears a jacket and pants by Regina Pyo and earrings by COS. Samara wears a jacket and a skirt by Regina Pyo and a bag from Carole Tanenbaum Vintage Collection.

Above. Samara wears a suit and shirt by Beaufille, a bag by Hugo Boss and earrings from Carole Tanenbaum
Vintage Collection. Madison wears a shirt by Wooyoungmi, a blazer by The Row and a skirt by Victoria Beckham. Right: Samara
wears a coat and shirtdress by Fendi and a scarf and earrings by Hermès.

Advice to ease the tricky bits of intimacy. Photography by *Aaron Tilley* & Styling by *Sandy Suffield*

1:   Know Yourself

INTIMACY

How to become acquainted with yourself more intimately.

"There's a huge difference between examining and dwelling," says Lori Gottlieb, the LA-based psychotherapist behind *The New York Times* bestseller *Maybe You Should Talk to Someone*. Gottlieb—whose book interweaves the crises of her patients with her own reckoning with therapy—is decidedly against navel-gazing. Instead, she advocates therapy as a tool for personal progress. Likening her role of therapist to that of editor, she explains how she helps patients reshape their own narrative through self-examination.

PU: *When someone comes to see you, what are you looking out for?* **LG:** I like to say that that I'm listening for the music under the lyrics. The lyrics are, "Here's why I came today," and the music is, "What's the underlying struggle or pattern that got you into this situation in the first place?" And that's often what we end up working with. We all have blind spots and it's really hard to see your own. Whatever those blind spots are, there's usually something very tender there that's hard for us to look at. It takes another person to help you, very gently, see what they are so that you don't keep stepping in the same puddle over and over.

PU: *Does it ever serve us to remain in a state of blindness?* **LG:** Generally, people who choose not to look at something that is important in their lives end up having some kind of symptom. It's not like you can just say, "I'm going to pretend that this doesn't exist." Feelings need air—and so eventually they'll come out. They might come out in destructive behavior, self-sabotage, relational difficulties, insomnia, depression, anxiety, irritability—all kinds of ways that the person might not recognize as being related to whatever they're willfully not looking at. The people who tend to live with the most inner peace, and who navigate the world most smoothly, are those who say, "I want to understand myself and the people around me because I will live a more fulfilling and meaningful life."

PU: *How do you guide someone through this process of self-examination?* **LG:** I help them listen to their story a little bit differently. As we start to revise their story, we find that certain characters in the story should be minor characters instead of major; we look at their own role in the story; we consider if somebody else were telling the story how they'd understand the problem. It's about holding up a mirror to somebody and helping them to see themselves in a way that they ordinarily don't.

PU: *For self-understanding to deepen, what other narratives must we let go of?* **LG:** I always say that therapy isn't just about getting to know yourself, it's also about getting to un-know yourself. It's about un-knowing these stories that are holding you back and getting to know who you really are. I think most people are very pleasantly surprised when they start to get to know themselves as an adult.

PU: *If someone is reluctant to try therapy, what advice would you offer?* **LG:** I think the biggest misconception is that you're going to go to therapy, you're going to talk about your childhood ad nauseam, and you're never going to leave. And that's just not at all what the therapeutic experience is. It's very much about the here and now and what's happening in your life that's keeping you stuck. Try a session to see what it's like. If you leave that session and you ask yourself, "Did I feel understood? Was this person easy to talk to?" then you might go back again.

Words by Pip Usher

2: Talk Dirty

We are repeatedly told that clear communication about sexual desire is crucial to healthy relationships, while seldom being given any practicable frameworks or approaches to help us tackle that sticky task.

Asking for what we want in bed is hard. Our resolve to do so often falls flaccid because requesting something means admitting we want it. We've been culturally conditioned to view sex as dirty, shameful or taboo—especially any act that falls outside the mainstream patriarchal preoccupation with straightforward, straight penetration.

Vocalizing that we're intrigued by an X-rated fantasy risks incurring judgment. It requires bravery; and the stakes are arguably higher in long-term relationships, where there's the worry that our partner might interpret us coveting something different as a sign that what they've previously done has been wrong. We fear destroying their confidence, or even losing their trust. "Additionally, there's the misconception that if we have 'good chemistry' with someone and they're the 'right fit,' we shouldn't have to talk about what we like, because they'll just know," says psychosexual therapist Kate Moyle. While a well-matched partner may be able to intuit your passions to a limited extent, the future looks dim for those who conflate compatibility with clairvoyance.

Even when we do feel empowered to authoritatively express our true appetites, we may still suffer from what I call "the genie lamp problem." Just as Aladdin was confined to three wishes, we feel we must tightly cap the number of things we ask for between the sheets, lest we seem greedy or hard to please. We put up with a vibrator being used on an annoying pulsing setting, because our partner has already acquiesced to introducing a toy, plus taken instruction on how to angle it.

So, how to start having more comfortable, compassionate conversations with effective outcomes? One way to sidestep the danger of a lover feeling criticized is by "scapegoating." There are myriad variables that can legitimately render a type of stimulation that once felt good less pleasurable: stress, aging, or—for women—changes during the menstrual cycle, and contraception. You could lean on one of these to open a chat about how you've noticed your "body doesn't seem to be responding in the same way" to the usual routine. Yes, it's an excuse. But when we talk about how to talk about sex, perhaps we need to be honest, not idealistic, about the fact not everyone is ready for radical honesty.

Sinead O'Hare—co-founder of The Sway, a couples' subscription box service delivering curated collections of products, along with cue cards designed to start conversations about how both parties want to explore the contents—has another suggestion. "A good way to test how your partner might react to an idea you want to try is to describe an erotic dream you supposedly had about it," she says. "Chances are they'll find it hot, and you can use it as a jumping-off point, but you have the reassurance of being able to dismiss it as 'just a dream' and quietly reevaluate your next steps if they react unenthusiastically."

Adam Wilder runs House of Togetherness, a studio in London's Covent Garden offering workshops aimed at enhancing sexual mindfulness. He recommends couples take turns at a hands-on activity that will not only help hone their abilities to identify and fearlessly ask for what they crave, but also to pay better attention and react with grace to whatever may be asked of them. "In 'Bossy Massage,' the giver may only touch the receiver precisely when, where and how they ask them to," he explains. "The recipient practices reflecting on what they genuinely want, then requesting it accurately, whilst the masseur is prompted to notice where their instinct is to bulldoze in with more, hang back and give less, or make assumptions about what style of stroke their lover wants rather than enquiring."

This note to listen as well as talk is essential relationship advice. Whatever our sexual desires, be they more foreplay or a three-way, communications should always flow both ways.

How to open up about sexual desires. *Words by Alix Fox*

3: Phone Home

Words by Pip Usher

When social psychologist Susan Newman started research for her book *Nobody's Baby Now*, she observed the same causes of strife occurring between the 150 adult children that she interviewed: The problem was their parents. From parental scrutiny around choice of spouse to conflicting expectations of career to money issues, she realized that many adult children needed guidance on how to repair—and ultimately reinvent—a fractious relationship with their parents. Newman shares her advice on how to build a more meaningful and mature connection between the generations—and explains why, no matter our age, it's still worth asking our parents for advice.

PU: *Why do we end up stuck in destructive patterns with our parents?* **SN:** Both adult children and parents tend to slip back into their old roles. The adult child continues to act like their 10-year-old self, allowing their parents to influence, judge, and critique their lifestyle and partner and how they are raising their children. And the parents baby them, telling them what to do and essentially running their lives as they did when that adult child was young.

PU: *How can we change that?* **SN:** As an adult, you need to act like an adult. When your parents are being too critical or demanding, you can point this out. Often parents are in ruts: They're stuck where they were and they're not even aware of their own behavior. They're certainly not aware that this behavior upsets you. They're just continuing as they always have. Another thing that's helpful is to look at the humor in the situation and say, "This is ridiculous. I'm 35 and my parent is still telling me to go comb my hair."

PU: *Are there conversations that will help to strengthen our relationship as adults?* **SN:** Ask for your parents' help. As adult children, we spend a lot of time trying to get away from our parents commenting on our behavior and actions. But if you can ask them for advice, that will start new conversations and bring you closer together.

PU: *What about navigating topics that cause conflict?* **SN:** If, for example, you and your parents have differing political views, that would be a topic that you'd want to avoid. You can say to your parents, "Politics is off-limits. I'm not going to discuss that with you. We don't agree or, if we do agree, we go off on a tangent." You don't even have to be that explanatory. You can simply say, "Let's take politics off the table." That allows you, as the adult child, to avoid any confrontations or difficult conversations that you don't want to have.

PU: *If we can cultivate camaraderie with our parents, what do we stand to gain from it?* **SN:** It allows you to view your parents as people and not as mommy and daddy. That's the big win. You're forging a friendship with them that will go on for the rest of your lives. On top of that, you're building memories. It gives you an opportunity to discover mutual interests and learn family history. Your relationship becomes a new ball game where you can be thoughtful and inclusive both ways.

PU: *And how do our parents benefit?* **SN:** Parents get to see their adult children as people who have lives of their own. They get to see their strength. And they get to have this supportive structure that works two ways because, in most families, parents are going to be looking to their adult children for help as they age.

PU: *Is there one thing that parents wish their adult children understood?* **SN:** They want to be included in their child's life. They want to be supportive. But that's hard to do if tere are constant tensions and arguing or control issues still at work.

How to distinguish codependency from intimacy.   *Words by Debika Ray*

In 1987, psychiatrist Timmen L. Cermak proposed that "codependency" be included as a personality disorder in the American Psychiatric Association's handbook, the *DSM-III*. The APA rejected his proposal, concluding that, unlike substance addictions such as drug dependency and alcoholism, what's often referred to as "love addiction" is not an illness.

Nonetheless, the term has gained currency; now it's as much a subject of self-help books and magazine quizzes as relationship counseling and psychotherapy. *Cosmopolitan*'s "9 signs you're in a codependent relationship" listicle last year ran through a range of dysfunctional relationship dynamics that, to a greater or lesser extent, we've all witnessed and worried about in friends or in ourselves, including fear of abandonment and giving up hobbies or plans in order to be with a partner.

The term—believed to have its roots in the Alcoholics Anonymous movement—refers to a person in a relationship with an addict who sacrifices their own needs in favor of those of their partner. Co-Dependents Anonymous does not define codependence but paints a picture of behaviors in which someone makes their partner the center of their world, gaining validation by playing the role of martyr and savior, while encouraging dependence and dysfunction and enjoying the sense of control.

Domestic violence expert Carol A. Lambert notes that the label is frequently attached to women in abusive relationships who are manipulated into putting their partner's needs above their own. It is so often women who assume the mantle, having traditionally been raised to take on the role of uncomplaining, selfless caregiver and fixer, and taught that their role is to quietly, patiently and unconditionally support men, and gain satisfaction through self-sacrifice.

But several psychologists shy away from the term. Ann Smith, who has authored two books on the subject, argues in a blog post that the term has "evolved into a caricature of a passive victim, compulsive caretaker, controller, or enabler often blamed for causing the problem." "The truth is that what had been labeled in the past as codependency is actually human beings doing what comes naturally—loving," she writes.

Our tendency to pathologize unhealthy behavior when it causes emotional hardship aside, there is clearly something about codependence that's distinct from mere intimacy. As Shawn Meghan Burn, author of *Unhealthy Helping: A Psychological Guide for Overcoming Codependence, Enabling, and Other Dysfunctional Helping*, explains: "Codependence is an imbalanced relationship pattern where one partner assumes a high-cost 'giver-rescuer' role and the other the 'taker-victim' role." An incessant need to please arguably becomes a source of misery when it is exploited. And wanting your partner to make you feel valued is not the same as craving their validation in every way.

The clue to redressing the balance lies in the "co-", which makes it clear that this isn't something that can be treated in isolation as an individual problem or personal failure, but that codependency is inherently mutual.

5:   Go the Distance

Words by Daphnée Denis

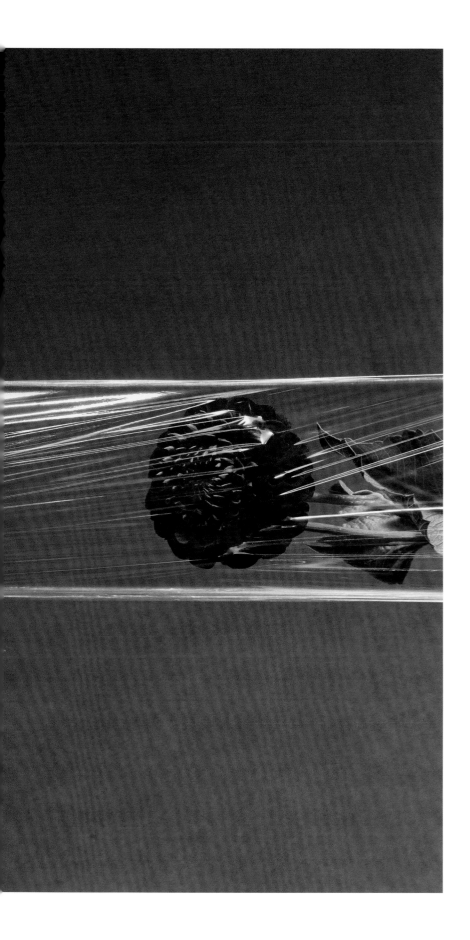

In Spike Jonze's movie *Her*, an artificial intelligence operating system (voiced by Scarlett Johansson) comes up with a somewhat perplexing idea in order to have real, embodied, sex with her lover, Theodore. She recruits a woman to act as her surrogate and "become" her body during sex. Theodore tries to follow through with the plan, but after a few minutes of kissing Isabella—the human facilitating their carnal relationship—he cuts the experiment short, deeming it "too strange."

The era of human/robot love may not be upon us yet, but people and smart devices are already engaging in this kind of three-way: Two humans in a long-distance relationship (be it friendly or more) can touch, or be intimate, through technology. Remote hugging machines, for instance, make it possible to embrace loved ones from a distance, thanks to connected torso-shaped cushions. And lovers missing each other's heartbeat can turn to Pillow Talk, a set of wristbands that will transmit the sound of their pulse to speakers under their partner's pillow. Remotely activated rings will vibrate to let someone know their sweetheart misses them.

There is little research on human response to haptic technology, which seeks to recreate the experience of touch. Still, these inventions are more disturbing than the possibility of human-robot intercourse: While the latter can be considered a fetish, much like using sex dolls, the former implies that something we perceive as intrinsically human—building an intimate bond—can be successfully performed by a machine.

For Dr. Markie Twist, a human development professor at the University of Wisconsin-Stout and author of T*he Internet Family: Technology in Couple and Family Relationships*, there is nothing new about humans bonding with objects: Just as children become emotionally attached to stuffed toys that "don't love them back," adults now develop feelings for their technology, even experiencing separation anxiety when parted from it.

The question isn't so much whether these devices can effectively substitute for human interactions (getting a hug from a pillow, however smart it may be, will never feel exactly the same as a human embrace), but rather whether our attachment to the technology itself goes beyond the connection we have to the live person operating it. Instead of merely facilitating the link between two people by mimicking human presence, a machine could become an integral part of the relationship it's being brought into—each person developing a unique bond with it, separate from the one they have with each other. In the upside-down world imagined by Spike Jonze, where the surrogate providing affection for an enamored AI system is human, the shifting dynamic is evident: Bringing a third party into the relationship changes it altogether. What if technology could do the same?

Archive:
Jackie Collins

Sex "sold" for *Jackie Collins*, but it was the emotional honesty of her writing that kept readers hooked for almost half a century. *Alexandra Heminsley* considers the enduring legacy of Hollywood's naughtiest novelist.

For a woman so associated with sex and decadence, Jackie Collins' day-to-day routine would have surprised many of her fans. She worked, writing in longhand with a black felt-tip pen, every day until her death in 2015. She went to bed early. She filed promptly. According to Suzanne Baboneau, managing director of Simon & Schuster UK and Collins' line editor since 1980, she "knew the value of a deadline, and always delivered a wonderfully clean manuscript."

Although Collins—with her Armani pantsuits, her panther-bedecked desk, and her iconic house designed to look like David Hockney's *A Bigger Splash*—epitomized Hollywood glamour to so many, she was in fact a hardworking Brit who, as Baboneau puts it, had "a real morality about her."

Born in Hampstead in 1937, she was brought up with her sister (the actress Joan Collins) on London's Marylebone Road. Her father was a theatrical agent, and she would regularly listen in on him and his friends discussing the women in their lives over card games. "From an early age I got the impression of the double standard, and I have been writing about it ever since," she told *The Guardian* in 2011.

This sense of being an observer—in the room but one degree removed from the action— stood her in good stead throughout her life. Collins moved to California in her early 20s to live with Joan, who was making a mark for herself in Hollywood. But Jackie didn't enjoy life in front of the camera, preferring to watch the machinations of the industry from afar while nursing her ambition to write.

She was in the habit of starting novels and abandoning them, only completing one once she had the encouragement of her second husband, Oscar Lerman, a nightclub impresario and founder of Tramp on London's Jermyn Street. Collins' first marriage had been stormy, ending after four years. Her husband had been bipolar and died of an overdose not long after they parted. But when Lerman read a few pages of what would become *The World is Full of Married Men*, he pushed her to complete it. The novel was an immediate bestseller, shocking and delighting audiences in equal measure. Each of the 31 novels that followed also became *New York Times* bestsellers, her sales eventually topping 500 million. She also helped her sister's career by writing the novels that would land Joan iconic roles in *The Stud* and *The Bitch*.

What was it that enabled this increasingly straitlaced figure, married to Lerman for over 26 years, to write such raunch? She fuelled the boom in "shopping and fucking" novels of the 1970s and '80s, and continued to ride that wave for decades. She blithely bypassed sub-

Photography: Earl Leaf/Michael Ochs Archives/Getty Images. Overleaf, Photograph: John Pratt/Keystone Features/Getty Images

sequent publishing trends including the family dramas popular in the '90s and the chick lit boom of the 2000s, not only taking her original readers with her but finding a new generation too.

One explanation for Collins' enduring popularity was her genuine passion for storytelling. She cited Dickens as an early inspiration and longtime favorite. "I loved the fact that he had all those different characters," she explained. A Dickensian love of colorful characters and far-fetched plot twists was something she successfully replicated within her own genre, says Baboneau. "She wrote dense, layered novels. She was a proper plotter. You can put people in Versace or Gucci or whoever but you can't pull it off for 30 books if that's all you've got."

Authenticity was also a key factor. "The sex in her books was real," explains Nigel Stoneman, her long-standing UK publicist. "She used to smile and say that she never wrote about anything she hadn't done herself, witnessed or had been told firsthand." This policy didn't leave her short of options: From her early forays into Hollywood living (including a teenage affair with Marlon Brando), to her later seat at the bar in Tramp, she had a truly peerless view of life behind the velvet ropes of LA and beyond.

Yet no matter how eye-poppingly filthy her sex scenes got, one thing her female characters all had in common was that—like Collins—they were hard workers. "Her heroines were not in the kitchen or the shops all day, they were out there running hotel complexes and movie studios," says Stoneman. "Those characters had things to do every day beyond falling love," agrees Baboneau.

This ambition in her female leads left the falling in love—and, of course, the sex—to be just that. Free from a quest for courtly knights or wealthy businessmen to look after them, her heroines' romantic lives shimmered with self-expression, emotional release and wild passion. She never skimped on detail. While the white-sheeted sophistication of '90s literature and the gawky comedic bunk ups of the new millennium sailed by, Collins was there with pages of sweat, flexibility and flesh slapping on tanned flesh.

She did it all without a trace of irony. Where so many other genres can only engage with women's sexual selves from beneath a veil of either cynical humor or furrowed academia, Collins took these wom-

en—and the women reading about them—seriously.

Their passions mattered to her, and her readers knew it. Collins' heroines were what readers wanted to be on their very best days.

Summer 2019 saw *Three Women* held up as a groundbreaking examination of female desire. Where many saw a "must read" nonfiction book of the year, filled with revelations about women's sexuality, others saw the ground covered as dispiritingly well-trodden, the women chronicled so very preoccupied by male desires. I fell more in the latter camp, having learned at the altar of Lady Collins: My teenage self felt something truly radical on reading the opening pages of *Lovers and Gamblers* as our heroine Dallas is introduced. She's admiring her own bikini-clad body in a full-length mirror prior to taking the stage at the Miss Los Angeles beauty pageant. Without a flicker of anxiety, she thinks to herself that she "deserved to win. There really was no contest." There was—and still rarely is—anywhere else on the literary landscape where women are so uninhibited in not just their desire but their delight in their own bodies.

Collins herself did not work out—a bit of swimming and table tennis being all she would admit to—and did not seem to feel any pressure to conform to the highly specific California aesthetic. When pressed by *The Guardian*, she responded, "I must be incredibly confident, because I've never felt that. You see these women and men—the whole plastic surgery thing—and they've got these little fat cheeks, they look like chipmunks. And you're like, 'Why are you doing that? What's the purpose?' I don't get it. Perhaps it's an English thing."

Perhaps it *was* an English thing. Like Hockney, whose *A Bigger Splash* she was so frustrated never to be able to buy, she somehow managed to be as British as fish and chips while creating art that glistened with LA exoticism. "When I was a kid growing up, I used to read my father's *Playboy* and I'd see these guys and they had fantastic apartments and cars. I have all of that now," she told the Associated Press in 2011. And yet every time Collins landed in the UK, Baboneau tells me, she "made a beeline to M&S Marble Arch for prawn sandwiches and then Boots for a top up of No7 Protect & Perfect." She really did know what women want.

Things

Love's a well-learned pas de deux. Even if the feelings fade, the steps still feel familiar.

Fall Apart

Photography by Pelle Crépin & Styling by David Nolan

Above: Webster and Abdou wear knit tops by DAKS. Right: Webster wears trousers by Dsquared2. Abdou wears a blazer by Brunello Cucinelli and trousers by Dunhill. They both wear a coat by Katharine Hamnett and shoes by Crockett & Jones. Previous spread: Webster wears a jacket and trousers by Hermès. Abdou wears a jacket and trousers by Celine.

Abdou wears a shirt and trousers by Margaret Howell and shoes by Crockett & Jones.
Webster wears a shirt by Turnbull & Asser, trousers by Paul Smith and shoes by Crockett & Jones.

Left: Abdou wears a shirt and waistcoat by Dunhill. Webster wears a shirt by Xu Zhi. Above: Abdou wears a shirt by Frank Foster and trousers by Xu Zhi.

Abdou wears trousers by Katharine Hamnett and a belt by Brunello Cucinelli. Webster wears trousers by Connolly.

BEYOND MONOGAMY

TEXT:
STEPHANIE D'ARC TAYLOR

First there were two. Then there were three, four, or however many partners a shared Google Calendar could schedule. But what does intimacy look like for the growing number of couples who choose to open up to sexual, or even romantic, relationships with others? Stephanie d'Arc Taylor goes fishing in the brave new world of nonmonogamy and discovers that with great freedom comes great responsibility, and a whole lot of talking.

Intimate relationships as our grandparents knew them, whether platonic, romantic or purely sexual, don't work anymore. A quest for efficiency has powered society's economic miracles since the Industrial Revolution, but the accelerated, relentless 20th-century streamlining of our lives also made us too busy for everyone but our nearest and dearest, and sometimes even for them. In recent decades, marriage rates in rich countries have plummeted; having grown up in a milieu of unhappy marriages, young people are increasingly saying "I don't."

The story is more complicated than that, though. Just because many of us aren't marrying doesn't mean we're not committing. Today we feel freer than ever to pursue our sexual desires—a path that was largely forged by last century's LGBT bravehearts who demanded the right to live and love openly. We're also increasingly experimenting with various partnership configurations. Curiosity about ethical nonmonogamy—the catchall term to describe polyamorous, multi-partner and nonexclusive relationships based on honesty—has reached a fever pitch, according to Google Trends data,

myriad think pieces and Dan Savage, the author, podcaster and sex advice columnist who has become a leading advocate for nontraditional couplings.

"The idea of intimacy has evolved away, thank God, from the notion that there is one kind of relationship that is good for everyone," he says, on the phone from Seattle. "People are increasingly empowered to make their own choices about all sorts of things that we weren't in the past allowed to make choices about. More and more, it's hard for people to pretend that there is just one way to have a healthy, functional relationship."

At his practice in London, psychosexual therapist Silva Neves has also noticed an uptick in clients seeking support within polyamorous or open relationships. "People are more aware now that there are different ways of being in relationships other than monogamy," he says. "It's more talked-about and less 'on the dark side' so more people are opting for it."

For many who have thought deeply on the subject, the question we should ask seems not to be "Why is nonmonogamy becoming a thing now?" but instead, "Why have we told

ourselves for so long that monogamy was our only option?"

Many believe that humans are not a species naturally disposed to lifelong pairings. "Like bonobos and chimps, we are the randy descendants of hypersexual ancestors," write Christopher Ryan and Cacilda Jethá in their book, *Sex at Dawn*. "Conventional notions of monogamous, till-death-do-us-part marriage strain under the dead weight of a false narrative that insists we're something else."

Our modern pace of life—accelerated over the 20th century from ambulatory to broadband speed—no longer allows us to wander down to the agora to do the shopping and flirt with acquaintances from the neighboring hamlet. Gone are the preindustrial salad days, when people had their panoply of needs met by a variety of community members. Parents and elders provided advice and the comfort of a good yarn; cousins and colleagues were ready for a conspiratorial giggle or ideological debate. Spouses were there at the end of the day for a cozy snuggle in bed. Everyone helped out with parenting. And, if you take it from Friedrich Engels, the German philosopher and close colleague of Karl Marx, everyone had sex with everyone. Before the capitalist system of private ownership was firmly entrenched in the 18th century, he believed, societies owned property collectively and existed in a "promiscuous horde" where there were no restrictions on sexual relationships.

Somewhere along the way, we went astray, corrupted by the power sex holds over us. Some argue that religion and the patriarchy developed to control sexuality—in particular, that of women. "There's the desire to control—and the impulse to channel—sex," says Savage. "Concurrent with that is the desire to own and control women. This is mixed up with so much of our cultural baggage about sex, mixed up with insecurity about paternity and fear of infidelity, which led to women being owned and sexually controlled in this way that men weren't because men made the rules."

As we begin to better understand—and reject—systems of patriarchy, it seems reasonable that monogamy is also coming under scrutiny. We increasingly recognize that the nostalgic, Norman Rockwell-esque image of a spouse who excels at work, scrubs the toilet dutifully according to a rota, concerns themselves with the children's vegetable intake, and remains intellectually stimulating and a freak in the sheets over the course of a decades-long partnership is unrealistic.

Opening up a relationship to new partners may seem a logical solution to a staid sex life,

"Intimacy, simplified, is about being seen and acknowledged in the here and now. If your partner is having those moments with other people, it encourages you to stop taking them for granted."

but it's not as easy as making a couple's profile on OkCupid. Monogamy is deeply woven into our sociocultural fabric, and going against the grain takes work. "If you really want to be intimate and have good relationships with every single partner, it takes a lot of time and a lot of effort," says Neves. "When you open a relationship to nonmonogamy, you need regular reviews," Neves continues. "Every six months, decide what's working and what's not working. It's an ongoing process of keeping in touch with yourself and your partners, to continue thinking about what you're doing and whether it's still working."

But more important—and much more difficult—than examining the relationship is understanding ourselves, what we like and what we're looking for. Parsing what we actually feel and what we think we're supposed to feel can be an issue as well, given that traditional notions of love often come with ideas of possession. Jealousy "absolutely comes up" with the couples Neves works with, he says. But he points out that jealousy is usually to do with self-esteem rather than what a partner may or may not be doing. "It's a good idea to do a lot of self-care and self-development and to be confident that even though your partner may have contact with other people, when your partner has contact with you, you're good enough."

The idea that humans collectively practiced monogamy in the centuries between the advent of monotheistic religion and 2011, when Savage first coined the term "monogamish" to refer to more sexually flexible relationships is, of course, preposterous. In her book *Marriage, a History*, Stephanie Coontz describes how 18th-century American men of a certain class would write to their wives' brothers about their mistresses. And affairs occur in 40% to 76% of modern marriages, according to researchers at the University of Texas at Austin.

This type of nonmonogamy—furtive infidelity—is assumed to be both the symptom and the cause of bad relationships, and painful for everyone involved. But "sometimes cheating is the least worst option," says Savage. For example, he received an email from a woman who was the primary caregiver for two children with special needs and financially dependent on a spouse who was sexually uninterested in her. "It's easy to say cheating is always wrong, but... I believe we can prioritize relationships over ideals. In the real world, sometimes to save a valuable relationship, that outweighs the value of the ideal of monogamy; cheating not only happens but has to happen." Savage continues, "Sometimes honesty is sadism. Sometimes the most loving thing you can do for your partner is to omit, or even actively lie."

The prevailing academic wisdom is that nonmonogamous relationships enjoy increased intimacy, because they force participants to be more honest with themselves and their partners. (Neves points out that members of the more frequently nonmonogamous gay community have been having these conversations for decades.) Of course, scheduling can be an issue: Many couples have leveraged tools like shared Google Calendars to keep track of their dating lives. The app allows details of events to be shared, or simply for participants to see when someone is free or busy. Neves also counsels primary partners to set up rules for what is and isn't allowed. But in practice it may be a different story; according to nonmonogamists, rules involving protection, or certain sex acts, are easy to break in the moment, or when feelings get involved.

The secret to a successful relationship, it seems, is the same whether or not its participants have sex outside it. "It's this thing in our culture," Neves says. "Once commitment happens, you think you can stop thinking about it. So much is unspoken: sex, relationships, boundaries. People can be living together for years in a relationship that doesn't work and isn't alive because they haven't reviewed or talked about it. One lesson that the nonmonogamous community can teach the monogamous community is to talk about it. When you are in a relationship, it's really important that those discussions are ongoing to avoid breaking someone's heart unintentionally."

"Intimacy, simplified," says Neves, "is about being seen and acknowledged in the here and now. If your partner is having those moments with other people, it encourages you to stop taking them for granted."

Eat Your Feelings

There's no place like home, and no taste like the food we associate with it. Photography by *Gustav Almestål*,
Set Design and Food Styling by *Niklas Hansen* & Fashion Styling by *Martin Persson*

Above: Coat and trousers by Bottega Veneta. Plate by HAY. Left: Dress by Stine Goya. Plate by HAY. Previous Left: Dress by Dagmar. Bowl by Höganäs Keramik and plate by HAY. Previous Right: Top by Rodebjer. Jacket and trousers by Ivy & Oak. Plate by Iittala and spoon by HAY.

Above: Dress by Acne Studios. Bowl by Arket. Left: Sweater by Tommy Hilfiger. Chair by Magis. Plate by Zara Home.

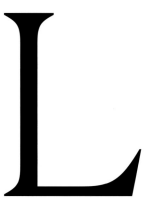

I   L

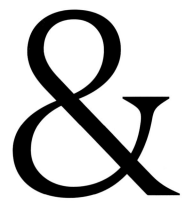

&

Love, trust and erotic leatherwear:
Stevie Mackenzie-Smith meets the married couple behind Fleet Ilya.

Words by
Stevie Mackenzie-Smith

Photography by
Iringó Demeter

E   S

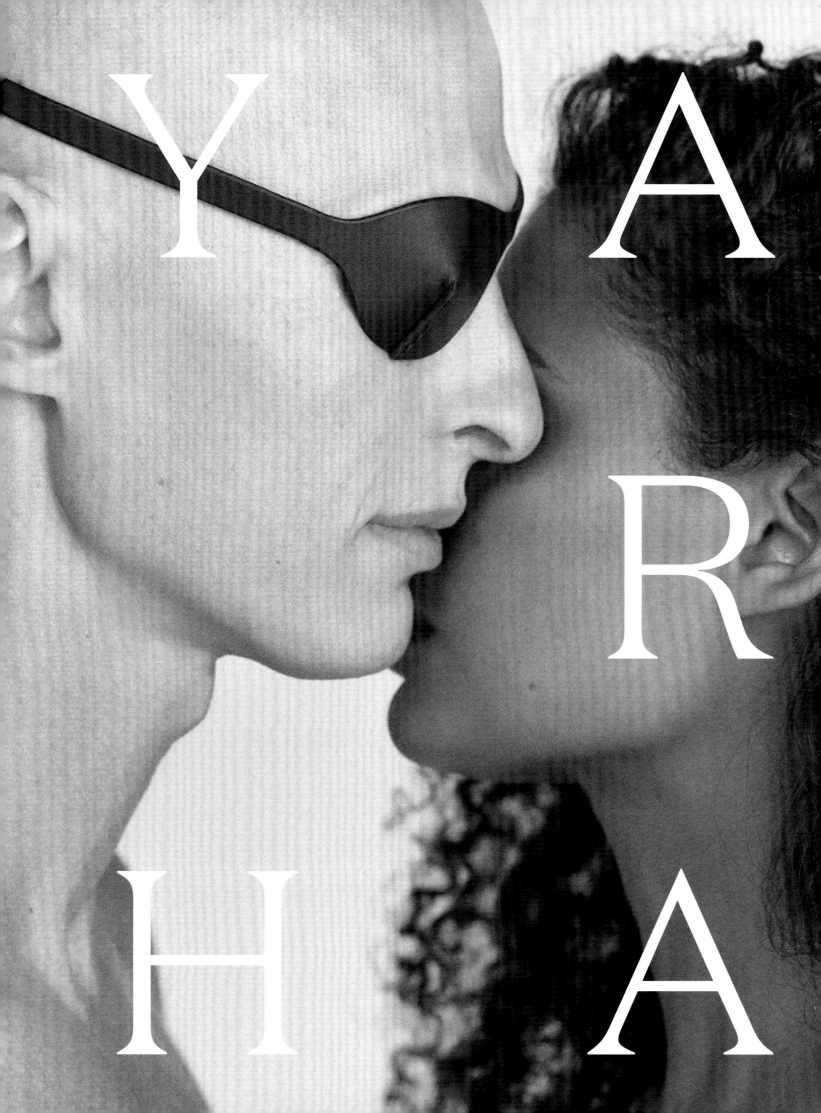

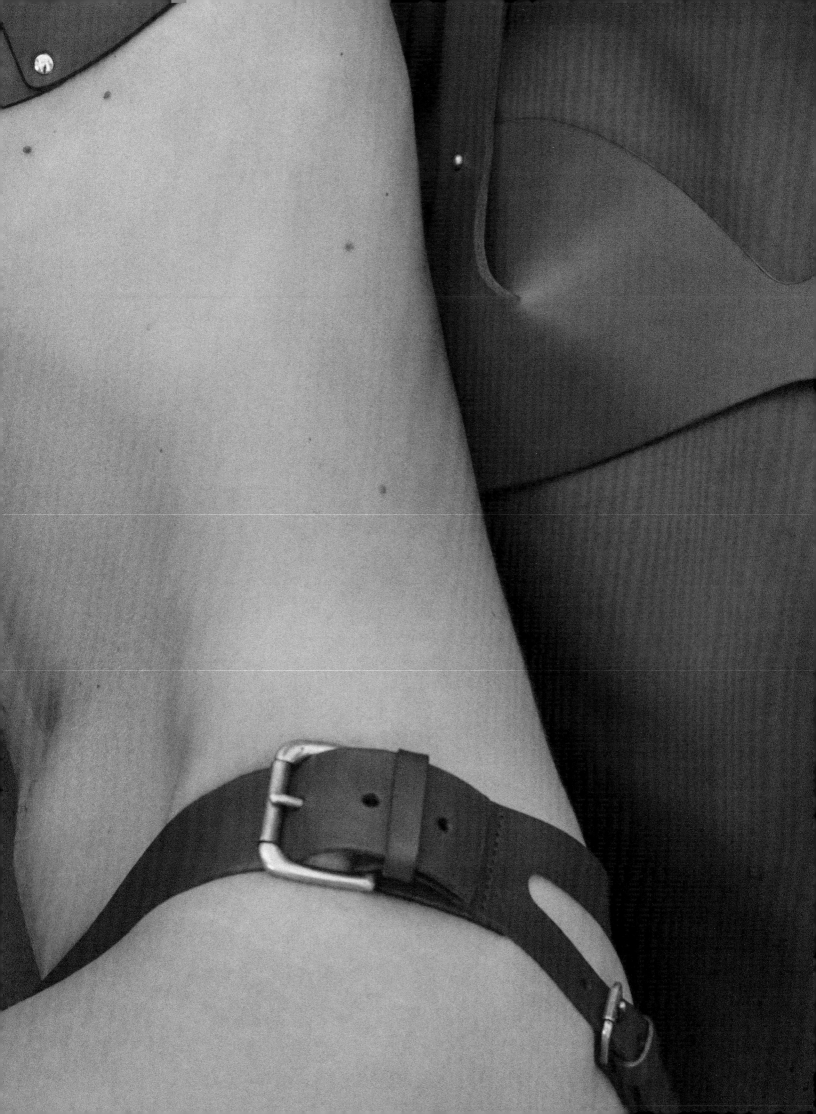

Hair: Hirokazu Endo, Makeup: Helena Kastensson, Photo Assistant: Jessica Ellis

"We often find that we're in conversation with people about really sexually intimate things."

It is late summer in London, which is to say that hot buses are full of wet necks and upper lips, corner shop ice-cream freezers are low on the good stuff, and the intermittent rain showers still call for the carrying of an umbrella. It's the perfect time to get away. Resha Sharma and Ilya Fleet are just back from France, and have the laid-back, contemplative air of two people who've been spared negotiating a hot city in the summer. They hitchhiked through parts of Normandy, landing at a quiet farmhouse in Aquitaine. It's quite a change from Dalston—home to the atelier from which they've run their luxury subversive leatherwear label, Fleet Ilya, for over 15 years.

They visited a nudist colony, where naked families biked together and mundane business transactions took place in the buff. Sharma remembers a young ice-cream seller who looked like a "Pre-Raphaelite painting," but the older bodies made an impression too. They have left her thinking about different creative directions they could take with the brand's editorial photography; currently Fleet Ilya's Instagram feed leans toward a moody and austere kind of beauty, with lithe, harnessed bodies arranged on modernist chairs. "People were so confident, and all looked so different," Fleet says. "It was a very liberating place."

Fleet was born in Ukraine and brought up in an artistic household in Jerusalem, where being around unclothed life models was a regular part of his childhood. He recalls an early understanding of transience—he remembers his sister rushing to tell him about the nearby Chernobyl nuclear disaster when he was four, and how people stopped drinking tap water and eating fresh vegetables and fruit. His father, who lost family and friends to the Holocaust, devoted his adult life and artwork to commemorating the atrocities of war. How did those early impressions affect him? "It makes you realize that anything could happen, and life is now," he explains.

He first became interested in the yielding potential of leather when he was a waiter working above a leather supplies shop. Used to helping his sculptor father lug unwieldy, monumental sculptures from studio to gallery, leather seemed a forgiving and functional material in comparison. He started to make small, practical accessories like lighter holders and cigarette cases. After moving to London at 20 he studied saddle-making. He commuted weekly to a small town just outside Coventry—once the land of naked rider Lady Godiva—taking long, winding bus journeys through the countryside to learn from the best. "He was very patient," says Fleet, remembering his teacher. "He taught me my very bad English and we somehow managed!" He learned how to smooth and bevel, how to get a saddle to sit close but comfortably on a horse.

Sharma, who grew up in West London, remembers as a child being struck by how different her parents were from each other. Her father was the liberated "party animal," while her mother was "not at all open with her body." She turns to Fleet in the chair beside her, and over the sound of the August rain pummeling the studio's plastic corrugated roof, she observes: "Within your family, the body wasn't something to be ashamed of or hidden." It was, she believes, what drew her to Fleet and his creative upbringing.

Fleet and Sharma met in the early 2000s at Nag Nag Nag, a notorious electro night thrown every Wednesday at Soho-based queer club Ghetto. Run by Jonny Slut, it celebrated self-expression and sexual fluidity. Boy George was a regular, as was the community of messy freaks and art students who barely batted a neon lash if they bumped into Kate Moss in the bathroom.

"It was quite a moment when we met," Sharma says, remembering the gravitational pull toward the enigmatic stranger who was "wearing sunglasses in a club—it was ridiculous!" (Today, Fleet wears a navy T-shirt, sturdy white jeans and Nike sneakers; Sharma is in an elegant cream-colored safari jacket—the discerning uniforms of busy people with good taste.) At the time, Sharma was a student at Central Saint Martins and Fleet was selling handmade belts and bracelets to Soho's independent sex and fashion shops. "It wasn't like it is now," he explains, "many of them belonged to families and were very welcoming." He could often

be spotted walking through Soho with a roll of leather on his shoulder. "Ilya was almost like a cult leader at the time with his vision," says Sharma. "He was so driven. I really believed in him." They joined forces after she graduated, drawing on Sharma's training in visual design to make erotic leatherwear that communicated the freedom, tolerance and self-expression they'd found within the Nag Nag Nag community.

They worked with brown leather and brass, in contrast to the glossy black and silver fetish wear that dominated Soho shopfronts. The newly opened sex boutique Coco de Mer became an exclusive stockist, Sienna Miller wore one of their harnesses over a black woollen riding coat. Fashion magazines found that these designs—paired with covered skin and froufrou dresses—were a way to soften the taboo of bondage wear. Through trial and error, and without formal training or pattern cutting skills, Fleet applied saddlemaking principles to leather fitted for the human body. He made wearers feel comfortable and safe—but powerful and sexy too—in smooth, flexible leather, like a second skin.

They worked tirelessly, often through the night. "It was blood, sweat and tears for many years," Sharma explains. "We challenged each other in a way that we wouldn't in a platonic partnership. We pushed each other as creatives and as individuals." Fleet adds: "We didn't have parents who could support us—we both felt a responsibility to help our families, especially because they weren't doing great at the time."

Fleet Ilya offered a new, refined kind of fetish wear, distinguished by the absence of seediness. It could be worn in bondage play, or as sartorial accessories in high-end nightclubs. The collection gave people the chance to wear a private side of themselves out in public. "Just by existing [as a brand], I feel like we've given a lot of people freedom, even within our social circle," says Sharma. "We often find that we're in conversation with people about really sexually intimate things, because of what we do."

People's readiness to open up about their experiences, or attach explicit photographs to heartfelt emails of thanks, revealed to Sharma and Fleet the lack of opportunity for sex to be talked about honestly and openly. The harnesses, the strap-on underwear and saddles were providing customers with a deeper level of intimacy they might not have experienced before. "The action of closing a collar or closing the lock, dressing or undressing—it's a big part of prolonging the [sexual] experience. It makes it a ceremony, a ritual. It makes it serious, intimate and involved," Fleet explains. "Sometimes submitting is the most powerful thing," says Sharma, "It's freeing."

One client wrote to tell them about the life-changing power of their strap-on. They find deep fulfillment in these exchanges. "I love people," Fleet explains, "I love knowing where they've come from, what they're doing and their capabilities. I want to make things for them to be useful."

It's easy to see why people open their hearts up to them. They have a magnetic, almost spiritual energy that's stimulating to be around. Later, over a take-out box of onion rings, Fleet talks of the time they motorcycled around India, conjuring an image of the two of them, hair whipping around, holding each other in forward motion. The tolerance that launched their business has helped them grow as a unit too; it's the grit that keeps propelling them.

Fleet Ilya exists at the center of an unusual Venn diagram, at home in both high-end fashion magzines and fetish clubs.

4
Directory

CHARLES SHAFAIEH

Cult Rooms

Francis Bacon harvested his master works from the chaotic "compost" of his West London studio.

When the Irish-born artist Francis Bacon settled in London in the late 1920s, he was known not as a painter but as an interior designer. *The Studio* magazine described the 20-year-old transplant as "a young English decorator who has worked in Paris and in Germany for some years and is now established in London." An accompanying photo spread featured designs that exuded the clean, minimalist style that was popular at the time and which would become a recurring motif throughout his painting oeuvre. The spare aesthetic stands in marked contrast, however, to the self-described chaos which defined Bacon's longtime studio at 7 Reece Mews in South Kensington that he occupied from 1961 until his death in 1992. A few years later, the studio was painstakingly cataloged before being moved in its entirety—dust included—to Dublin's Hugh Lane Gallery.

"I work much better in chaos," Bacon commented, as if asserting a firm break from the trappings of his early, less fruitful, design career about which he spoke little, as well as the bourgeois, ordered respectability that dominated his childhood. "I couldn't work if it were a beautiful tidy studio. That would be absolutely impossible for me." In another interview, he declared that "chaos for me breeds images." Whether the mountain of material that filled the 12- by 14-foot studio birthed his paintings, or was merely the debris resulting from them, cannot be conclusively determined. What is undeniable is the assertive presence of 7,500 items strewn and piled throughout the rather petite space that feels that much more claustrophobic because of this too-muchness. Bacon acknowledged this. Speaking with his friend John Edwards, to whom he bequeathed the property, he called his home "a dump."

In preparing the move to Dublin, a team of archaeologists treated the detritus like layers of rock. They identified three distinct layers comprised of more than 570 books on topics ranging from Velázquez to the supernatural, 1,300 spare pages from other books, 200 magazines, 246 pieces of newspaper paraphernalia, 100 destroyed canvases (often with all figures cut out), 2,000 brushes and other painting tools, 70 drawings and 1,500 photographs—many of which were creased, folded and torn in ways that convey the plasticity and impermanence of flesh that Bacon captured in paint.

Among the other items are empty boxes of high-quality wine and Champagne that symbolize Bacon's drunken afternoons and evenings at bars with friends. Their presence alongside his brushes and paint are a kind of collapsing of his entire identity within the studio. The walls are noteworthy, too, as they were his testing ground for colors; he once referred to the patchwork of densely layered oils as his "only abstract paintings." Even the ceiling is splattered, a suggestion of the painter-as-dancer flinging brushes with abandon.

Deemed "compost" by Bacon, the mass of objects is often characterized by scholars as a physical manifestation of his unconscious—a vast accumulation from which allusions, inspirations, and direct action on the canvases can be traced. But this notion, like so many conjectures about art and artists based on studios and biographies, is unproductive, and arguably false. It was Bacon, after all, who brought this material, such as the photos he commissioned and from which he worked, into the room. He also spoke of having a distinct sense of where things were located. All of this suggests a more heightened awareness of his surroundings than some might believe, regardless of how messy they were.

Though the studio provides a glimpse at his predilections and working practices, like his work it fascinates as an enigma—a gesture toward something that resists classification. Bacon's paintings reside in a liminal space. In his description, he painted between illustration and abstraction; Gilles Deleuze wrote that the paintings have "no story to tell" and yet "something is happening all the same, something which defines the functioning of the painting." Something is happening in the room, too, even without the artist present. Yet without Bacon himself navigating the cramped space, any clear narrative cementing the room's link to his work is absent. As with the paintings, imposing connections and meaning is not just risky, it is a disservice to the impactful nature that both the work and studio exude in silence.

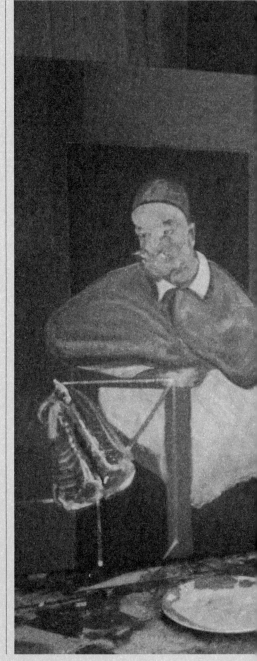

The HaaT creative director talks tradition, textiles and a half-century of collaborating with Issey Miyake.

CHARLES SHAFAIEH

Makiko Minagawa

For nearly three decades, *Makiko Minagawa* served under renowned designer Issey Miyake as textile director of the Miyake Design Studio. Then, in 2000, she launched her own brand, HaaT, under Issey Miyake Inc. The collection's name contains linguistic references to three essential themes of her creative philosophy: *HaaT*, Sanskrit for "village market," speaks to the collection's diverse spirit, from its eclectic use of textiles to the variety of aesthetic ideas it presents; *Heart* emphasizes the haptic and emotional qualities found in textiles; and *Haath*, Sanskrit for "hands," underlines the unity of Indian and Japanese craftsmanship at the collection's core. To mark Haat's showcase of *Khadi: Indian Craftsmanship*, an exhibition held at Issey Miyake's flagship store in New York's Tribeca in summer 2019, Minagawa discusses the importance of keeping craftsmanship alive.

CS: *How did your relationship with Issey Miyake begin?* MM: Around 1971, Mr. Miyake had just returned from Paris where he came up with the idea to make a collection using only textiles made in Japan but which would be comparable to the ubiquitous American blue jeans. I had just graduated from college, and it sounded like an interesting job so I started working for him, though not yet as a full-time employee. He didn't want to be influenced by other cultures, so I looked for various traditional, durable fabrics in Japan, such as a cotton used for lining men's kimonos and the soles of *tabi* [traditional socks]. Mr. Miyake wanted textiles that "no one had ever seen," but designing textiles is not his field of expertise. That's what he asked me to do.

CS: *For HaaT, you spend considerable time searching for local craftspeople. How do you develop those collaborations?* MM: There are so many unknown people with excellent craftsmanship out there. I love working with the people who I've discovered—inspiring each other and creating something together. It's crucial that these craftsmen carry on their art for future generations, which means someone has to give them work. We must support cultural inheritance. There is now an Issey Miyake store in Kyoto, and I feel I need to introduce craftsmanship from Kyoto, so I've been focusing on this more than ever. I also do similar collaborations each season with craftsmen from different regions of Japan.

CS: *For the exhibition* Khadi: Indian Craftsmanship *you've decorated Issey Miyake Tribeca with billowing roles of khadi. Why did you decide to focus on this particular fabric?* MM: I was inspired by the legacy of [the late Indian conservationist] Martand Singh. Nowadays so many fabrics are machine-made, and I wanted to go back to basics—the hand-spun, hand-woven fabrics that are the origin of all fabrics. Having an opportunity to explain about such heritage is important. There are so many cultural techniques in fabric making that need to be passed on.

CS: *What do you want people to notice about your collections?* MM: I want people to notice the details and unique textures. Of course color is important, but as long as there's sun and light, various textures are born. Whether it's embroidery or fringes, details give expression to a piece. Unlike untextured, machine-made garments flattened by ironing, these have subtle nuances. The story behind a garment also makes it stand out from the tons of clothing in the world. Sometimes it's difficult to communicate stories to the customer, but making garments for the sake of getting attention or recognition is not something that resonates with me. So I will just keep on explaining and telling the stories behind my pieces.

CS: *What type of progress are you focused on now?* MM: When I came to New York this summer, I learned a concept: "sharing" at a restaurant. In Japan, maybe because the portions are small, we don't use the word "share" for meals. I thought this idea of "sharing things with other people" could be applied to something else, too. For example, in the past, if the quality of a textile was not what we ordered, we'd reject it. But now, I think we need to utilize these textiles for something else. If the factory mistakes are unintentional, I'd like to give them life by creating something new, such as applying handiwork to them. It's a bit different from recycling; it's the notion of *mottainai* [regret over waste] in our culture.

This feature was produced in partnership with HaaT.

STEPHANIE D'ARC TAYLOR

Object Matters

A silly history of sausages.

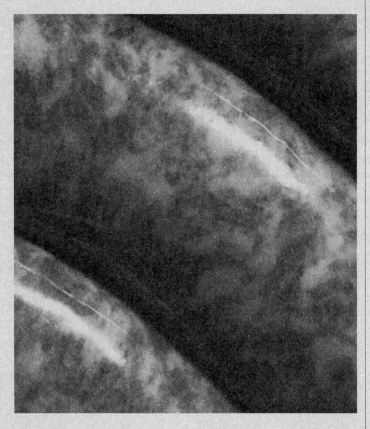

Humans may disagree on a lot, but we all love sausage. Whether you're snapping into the casing of an Armenian *sujuk*, a Cantonese *lap cheong*, a German *bratwurst* or a Chicago-style frankfurter, the basic idea—small pieces of animal protein, fat and seasoning stuffed into a tube—has remained virtually unchanged in the millennia since its inception.

The first discovery was that salt and smoke could keep meat fresh longer (the English word sausage derives from the Latin *salsus*, meaning "salted"). The next revelation was that undesirable casualties of the butchery process (entrails, viscera, skin, facial cartilage, connective tissue, etc.) could be made edible—and tasty!—when combined with chunks of fat and seasoning. And the final realization was all about efficiency: The whole thing could be conveniently packaged and easily transported within the (now empty) intestine of the same beast.

Back before you could visit an air-conditioned super-emporium to buy pre-butchered meat encased in white Styrofoam and clear plastic, animal flesh was expensive, awkward to handle and transport, and prone to becoming poisonous if not consumed quickly enough. Even after the 18th-century agricultural revolution, only the rich could afford to eat protein-rich meat regularly.

The proliferation of sausages made meat accessible to the urban working classes, who traditionally had neither the money to purchase fresh meat nor the facilities necessary to cook and serve it quickly enough. But sausage—delicious and delightfully shaped—was also soon embraced by the upper classes, including eventually Queen Victoria herself (who liked the meat to be chopped, not minced).

Eating animals may now be considered passé in certain circles, but we have hardly reached peak sausage consumption (which is, perhaps, regrettable for the prospects of our sizzling planet). It's such a popular food that even ethical vegetarians have sausage options from buzzy plant-based brands Beyond Meat and (soon) Impossible Foods.

Plant-based sausage might not turn into as great a social equalizer as its forebearer, but at least we won't mind so much watching them get made.

SPICE UP YOUR LIFE

by Pip Usher

A study has revealed the quickest way to find out the temperament of your date: Take them to an Indian restaurant, order a fiery vindaloo, and watch what happens next. It turns out that a lust for life often translates to a lusty appreciation of spicy food; those who enjoy the burn of a chili-heavy dish also tend to be extroverts, risk-takers and adrenaline junkies. A separate piece of research from the 1980s found a correlation between liking roller coasters and enjoying spicy food, suggesting that you really are what you eat. (Top: Macaron by Ladurée. Center: Lemon Squeezer by Petley. Bottom: Originale Dijon Mustard by Maille.)

Left Photograph: Gustav Almestål, Stylist: Pernilla Löfberg. Right Photographs: Courtesy of Ladurée, Everyday Needs and Maille

The director of a new documentary about romantic comedies pays homage to the genre's queen of hearts, *Nora Ephron*.

ELIZABETH SANKEY

Peer Review

I thought a lot about Nora Ephron when I was making my first film, *Romantic Comedy*. I thought about how, if the genre was held in the same esteem as thrillers or dark dramas, Ephron—who wrote and produced *When Harry Met Sally*, and wrote and directed *You've Got Mail*, *Sleepless in Seattle* and *Bewitched*—would be considered a titan, as lauded as Scorsese or Kubrick. But as romcoms are often dismissed or even derided—too fluffy, too feminine —those who make them are taken less seriously.

Even I had to reckon with my own internalized misogyny when diving into the subject. Romantic comedies encourage heteronormative values; they insist women be fixated solely on finding a partner. But perhaps the most problematic thing about them—other than their insipid whiteness and privilege—is that they work. I want more from life than a monogamous relationship, but that doesn't stop me crying when Harry knows Sally so well that her face scrunches up with tears. And my heart, which desires so much more than a big white wedding, cannot help but be broken and then remade every time I watch *Sleep-less in Seattle*, when Sam reaches for Annie's hand at the top of the Empire State Building.

Looking back, what I've always loved most about Ephron's protagonists is that they spend so much of their screen time without their suitors. In *You've Got Mail*, Kathleen only really meets NY152 (the username of her online love interest, Joe Fox) in the last scene. And in *Sleepless in Seattle*, Annie—despite obsessing about Sam for many months—doesn't speak to him until she's holding his son's teddy bear in those final moments.

As a young woman, it was thrilling to watch these heroines work out who they really are and what they really want before they're able, and allowed, to fall in love. And even when Ephron's characters do spend screen time together—Harry and Sally, for example— they're still both on a journey of self-discovery, changed by the circumstances of their lives, not by each other. Ephron taught me that so much of finding true love is the dialogue you have with yourself, the narrative you create in your own mind. And, most crucially, that you should never feel obligated to sublimate or change who you are in order to get it.

PIP USHER

Love Bombing

Beware too much, too soon.

In the 1970s, Korean cult leader Sun Myung Moon coined a term for the attitude assumed by "Moonies"—members of his crackpot Christianity spin-off, the Unification Church. "What face could better represent love than a smiling face? This is why we talk about love bomb; Moonies have that kind of happy problem," he said.

Beneath the attentive smile, however, lurked a sinister reality. After Moonies had identified a potential recruit, their love bombing—a technique of emotional manipulation in which a person is bombarded with flattering attention—began. One former recruit testified that he had only agreed to go along to his first meeting because he thought the women who suggested it were flirting with him. Two years later, he had become so deeply indoctrinated that his family hired defected former members to "deprogram" him.

Moon is not the only cult leader to rely on love bombing as a recruitment tool. Other dangerous opportunists, from the murderous Charles Manson to the Jonestown massacre mastermind Jim Jones, have seized upon it as a way to gain power over their followers. First, a vulnerable person is identified, preferably one who is iso-lated or struggles with low self-esteem. Then begins the courtship, an assault of affection and individualized attention that hinges upon our basic human need to feel significant. As the feigned warmth of these relationships lures the recruit in, extremist ideology can be introduced. Ultimately, the hope is that they will replace their network of friends and family with the cult.

Love bombing is also deployed by narcissists as they enter into a new relationship. A narcissist possesses an inflated sense of their own importance, a lack of empathy for others and a pathological need for admiration. Their grandiose belief in their own superiority motivates them to seek an acolyte—the role they expect their partner to fill.

In the early days of a relationship, a narcissist will rely on romantic gestures, a barrage of near-constant communication and talks about the future to overwhelm their target. With time, the displays of adoration will falter and in their place will appear control and degradation tactics to keep their partner obedient. Like a cult leader, there is a price attached to their attention. They expect their partner, through total capitulation, to pay it.

Left Photograph: Gustav Almestål, Set Design: Matilda Beckman. Right Photography: Courtesy of La Maison du Chocolat, Cousu de Fil Blanc and Astier de Villatte.)

PRESENT AND CORRECT

by Pip Usher

As many a disgraced politician can attest, there lies a crucial distinction between a business gift and career-wrecking corruption. A perusal of the gift policy of the British royal family—surely the experts on etiquette—suggests refusing anything that might place one under obligation to the donor. But can a gift ever be given without the hope of getting something in return? In short, no. Be it the anticipation of a reciprocal gift or else the more intangible benefits gained by increased goodwill, gifting inevitably comes laden with the expectations of any relationship-building exercise. So go ahead and accept the gift, give something back—and always draw the line at an envelope stuffed with cash. (Top: Opéra Scented Candle by Astier de Villatte. Center: Coffret Maison by La Maison du Chocolat. Bottom: Black Tea Soap by Cousu de Fil Blanc.)

Photograph: Alexandre Souêtre

ALEX ANDERSON

All Freak Out

The mystery of mass hysteria.

Sometimes we feel so deeply that it causes physical discomfort, a visceral reaction that transports emotion to the body's core. Immense joy takes the breath away; an awful sight induces nausea. An intense form of this relationship between mind and body is called "conversion disorder," in which stress or depression manifest as convulsing limbs, blindness, paralysis. The emotional condition converts into a physical one. Physicians used to call this strange psychologically driven illness "hysteria." Stranger still is mass hysteria, in which a group of people sicken from the same emotional trigger.

Imagine, as you ride the bus, a passenger steps off muttering threateningly. You smell something strange and catch the eye of another passenger who wrinkles her nose, frowning. Minutes later, the driver pulls over and is violently ill. Sweaty and gray, he asks if everyone is okay. Apparently not: You feel sick, and another passenger convulses with nausea, so the driver quarantines the bus until paramedics arrive. But they too succumb to the contagion. You and the other panicked passengers, fearing terrorism, wait to die, but everyone soon recovers. Such a scenario unfolded in 2004 on a bus in Vancouver, Canada. Mysteriously, health officials found no cause, so they diagnosed mass psychogenic illness—mass hysteria—triggered by shared fear.

Because we connect with each other emotionally, particularly under difficult circumstances, conversion disorders can move quickly from person to person. This happened on the bus in Vancouver. In 2011, it happened again among 19 students who began to twitch and shout unintelligibly at a school in western New York. Despite wild speculation about a toxic spill and government experiments, investigators could discover no environmental cause for the outbreak. The common root, it seems, was stress. Social and academic pressure manifested as tics and outbursts in one student, and stressed, empathetic friends soon involuntarily followed along. Other students learning about the outbreak via social media, suffered the same symptoms, adding a strange twist to an already bizarre outbreak. Medical sociologist Robert Bartholomew proposes that this case may demonstrate "a shift in the history of psychogenic illness, in which the primary agents of spread are the Internet, media, and social networking sites." That is to say, we might all be carrying an agent of mass hysteria in our pockets.

Add a touch of romance
to solve these clues.

ANNA GUNDLACH

Crossword

DIRECTORY

ACROSS

1. Mizrahi of fashion
6. Southern term of respect
10. Verb for voters and fishers
14. "Same here"
15. Stone of "The Favourite"
16. Tolkien monsters
17. Contempt
18. Active one
19. Fairy-tale monster
20. "It's gonna be a minute before I become the kind of person who attacks wind mills"?
23. Musical based on poems by T. S. Eliot
24. Lots
25. Ancient Germanic tribe who slayed with their standup?
30. Direction opposite WSW
31. Model's session
32. "Oh, give it ___"
34. What you used to be a long time ago?
35. Confronted head-on
37. Curve of the foot
41. Informal French greeting
43. Long-distance communication option

44. Barley wine or saison
47. Some of the performers on "Bovine Baywatch"?
50. River in a Strauss waltz
52. Asian sea that has almost completely dried up
53. Form of intimacy given to this puzzle's theme answers
57. Emmy-winning Falco
58. Bridge fee
59. Puts the kibosh on
62. Nevada city with lots of gaming
63. "Understood"
64. Bring to mind
65. Starter home?
66. Requirement
67. Get clean, in a way

DOWN

1. Bouncers check them
2. [that was their mistake, not mine]
3. Lots
4. Dreadfully terrible
5. Someone in your phone's address book
6. Gorgon with a stony gaze
7. Mine, in France
8. Visa alternative
9. Like the crew of the S.S. Minnow
10. Made like a pigeon
11. Diamond-shaped sweater pattern
12. What the title "Black Mirror" describes
13. Dangerous African fly
21. There are four in a gal.
22. Easy lob
25. OK clock setting
26. "Duh, now I get it"
27. Animal sound heard from a See 'n Say
28. Hobby knife brand
29. A lode off one's mine?
33. Use some vacation hours

35. Able to speak like a native
36. ___ cable
38. Bulleit variety
39. EMT's skill
40. "___ the DJ, I'm the Rapper" (1988 hip-hop album)
42. "Mamma Mia! Here We Go Again" inspiration
43. Squirreled away
44. Stick together
45. Heaped praise upon
46. Software for searching or graphics
48. In the post
49. Alums-to-be (abbr.)
51. Apply to
54. Medicine measure
55. "Twittering Machine" painter Paul
56. Hole for an SD card
60. Boxing win
61. Intimate subject

THE LAST WORD

The most romantic setting for intimacy may be a quiet beach at sunset, but the most common one will likely be a familiar bedroom after a long day's work. Sex advice columnist *Dan Savage*, interviewed on page 160, shares his advice for couples on becoming better bedfellows by treating sleeping spaces like living rooms.

I'm going to be a scold. I think having a neat, clean and tidy bedroom makes you excited to go there with your partner at the end of the day. Let one person take responsibility for it (maybe the other person gets the car serviced or takes the garbage out). If nothing else, it'll inspire you to have sex more. Why do we go on vacation and have sex every night? One of the contributing factors is that the housekeeper makes up the bed every day.

Bedrooms are often messy afterthoughts, because the only people who see them are the people who sleep in them. We keep kitchens and living rooms clean, but we get out of a messy bed in the morning and leave it all day. A well-organized space just really improves crawling into bed at night with your partner. The bedroom is the place where your respect for each other—and the value you place on each other and the relationship—is visually present. You wouldn't let people come over for dinner in a room that is a wreck. Your bedroom should be as well turned out when you want to have sex in it as the dining room is when you have people for dinner. It's more fun when you're taking that pristine clean space and messing it up.

håndværk

A specialist label creating *luxury basics*.
Ethically crafted with an unwavering
commitment to *exceptional quality*.

handvaerk.com

Stockists

3.1 PHILLIP LIM
31philliplim.com

ACNE STUDIOS
acnestudios.com

AMI PARIS
amiparis.com

ANDY WOLF
andy-wolf.com

ARKET
arket.com

BABATON
aritzia.com

BEAUFILLE
beaufille.com

BOTTEGA VENETA
bottegaveneta.com

BRUNELLO CUCINELLI
brunellocucinelli.com

CAROLE TANENBAUM
caroletanenbaum.com

CHLOÉ
chloe.com

CONNOLLY
connollyengland.com

COS
cosstores.com

CROCKETT & JONES
crockettandjones.com

DAGMAR
houseofdagmar.com

DAKS
daks.com

DE FURSAC
defursac.fr

DEREK LAM
dereklam.com

DSQUARED2
dsquared2.com

DUNHILL
dunhill.com

ELEVEN SIX
eleven-six.co

ELIE TAHARI
elietahari.com

EQUIPMENT
equipmentfr.com

EVERYDAY NEEDS
everyday-needs.com

FALKE
falke.com

FENDI
fendi.com

FRANK FOSTER
frankfostershirts.com

GABRIELA HEARST
gabrielahearst.com

GIUSEPPE DI MORABITO
giuseppedimorabito.com

HAY
hay.dk

HERMÈS
hermes.com

HUGO BOSS
hugoboss.com

ICICLE
icicle.com

IITTALA
iittala.com

IVY & OAK
ivy-oak.com

KATHARINE HAMNETT
katharinehamnett.com

LANVIN
lanvin.com

LAURA LOMBARDI
lauratlombardi.com

LOEFFLER RANDALL
loefflerrandall.com

MAGIS
magisdesign.com

MAISON SIMONS
m.simons.com

MARGARET HOWELL
margarethowell.com

MARTIN GRANT
martingrantparis.com

MARTINEZ
souliersmartinez.com

MAXMARA
maxmara.com

ORMAIE
ormaie.paris

ORSEUND IRIS
orseundiris.com

PAUL SMITH
paulsmith.com

REISS
reiss.com

ROCHAS
rochas.com

RODEBJER
rodebjer.com

SALLY LAPOINTE
sallylapointe.com

SANTONI
santonishoes.com

SOPHIE BUHAI
sophiebuhai.com

SPORTMAX
sportmax.com

STINE GOYA
stinegoya.com

THE ROW
therow.com

TOGA
toga.jp

TOMMY HILFIGER
tommy.com

TURNBULL & ASSER
turnbullandasser.co.uk

VICTORIA BECKHAM
victoriabeckham.com

WOOYOUNGMI
wooyoungmi.com

XU ZHI
xuzhi.co.uk

TF Design
Modern Designs in Resin

tf.design

tf

ISSUE 34

Credits

COVER
Photographer
Romain Laprade
Stylist
Camille-Joséphine Teisseire
Hair/Makeup
Taan Doan
Models
Johanna Defant at
Elite Milan
Anders Hayward at SUPA
Model Management

He wears a turtleneck by
Martin Grant and a coat by
Acne Studios. She wears a
turtleneck by Sportmax.

P. 64 – 75
Models
Johanna Defant
at Elite Milan
Anders Hayward at SUPA
Model Management
Location
La Chiesa Madre by
Ludovico Quaroni in
Gibellina Nuova, Sicily.

P. 124 – 131
Hair & Makeup
Ronnie Tremblay
Models
Madison Leyes
at Plutino Models
Samara Smith
at Plutino Models

P. 150 – 159
Casting Director
Sarah Bunter
Models
Webster at Nii Agency
Abdou at Nii Agency
Groomer
Mike O'Gorman
Photo Assistant
Benjamin Whitley

P. 164 – 169
Fashion Stylist
Martin Persson
Model
Anastasiia V at Röster
Image Treatment
Karin Eriksson

P. 170 – 176
Stylists
Resha Sharma
Ilya Fleet
Models
Bimpe at Premier Models
Maddy Taylor at Premier
Models

P. 178 – 179
Photograph
Douglas Glass

Special Thanks:
Ruth Ansel
Mako Ayabe
Bruno Feitler
Zeno Franchini at
Fondazione Manifesto
Nicolas Moore
The New School Archives
and Special Collections
The Richard Avedon
Foundation